i

"CEMENTING EXCELLENCE"

Handbook for 360-degree Excellence in Cement &
Building-Materials Sales Function

By

Dr. E Ravishankar

DEDICATION

I strongly believe that one power, pure and holy, beyond thoughts and comprehension, dictates and thus world moves; universe exists. Every atom and its energy in the universe are but the manifestation of this Almighty Power. All credits for enabling me to come out with this book belong to this Supreme Power, worshipped by the world through many names and forms.

FOREWORD

As a practising, multi-functional consulting professional for over four decades after post-graduating from IIM Ahmedabad, I am delighted to have been invited by the author, Dr E. Ravishankar, to write this Foreword for his maiden venture in book writing. Sharing BITS Pilani, as a common alma mater, as well as being colleagues at Holtec, I have witnessed, on innumerable occasions, his keen and thought-provoking insights in the domain of cement marketing & sales. It is this insight which he has effectively translated into what constitutes the contents of this publication.

The country – India, the industry – cement and the function – cement sales & marketing – are facing the challenges of steep growth, steeper competition and the imperative need to modernise and thus remain contemporary. The pressure, therefore, for sales staff to don holistic caps and remain relevant in the rapidly unfurling, digitalized environment, that values integrative acumen, is indeed overwhelming. As an example of integrative foresight, a sales person, I am personally familiar with, propounded and established, through assiduous research, the hypothesis that the market, he was catering to, unequivocally believed that darker coloured cement was stronger than the lighter coloured variety. This finding was subsequently communicated to upstream product designers who evolved a technological solution, which led to a surge in sales volume as well as price. Such examples abound – a vast compendium of dormant market hypotheses still exist, that once addressed – can result in sustained success. Who better than the frontally placed, sales person can address this dormancy!

This book is directed towards equipping sales personnel with value-added skills and attitudes, to buttress their current repertoire and enhance their effectiveness and efficiency in dealing with the evolving needs. In this endeavour, it spans the details of foundation building to achieve excellence, the nitty-gritties of the process to realize stellar performance and finally the determinants of accomplished leadership and enhancement of personal worth. Explaining with brevity, and yet with admirable lucidity, the intricacies of the downstream supply-chain structure, market segmentation & positioning, perspectives in pricing, the habits & values that sales staff need to either adopt or relinquish and a host of other success-recipes, the book also advocates the adoption of a unique, KDA-based, four-pronged approach towards achieving 360-degree excellence in sales. Additionally, it also specifies four non-negotiable qualities that are an absolute must in the arsenal of the successful sales person of tomorrow.

Such a book comes like a whiff of fresh air since a parallel treatise on the subject, possibly, does not exist! I would like to complement Dr Ravishankar for this pioneering effort and wish his book all success.

Saumen Karkun,
Deputy Managing Director,
Holtec Consulting Private Limited
(Consultants to the Cement Industries of over 90 countries)
Gurugram (India)
20 July 2019

PREFACE

Divine grace enabled to retain and regard the advice given to me by the Vice Chancellor (VC) of "Birla Institute of Technology and Science, Pilani", when I completed my doctorate. He reiterated me, "You have done doctorate coming from an industry background in this prestigious university. With all the experience and education, you should be of special value to your industry and the nation".

I asked myself the question, "Having been intensely involved for decades in the cement industry and thereby acquiring all the comforts of life, what have you done in return to the industry?" I could not give a convincing answer to myself. I was a bit sad that I have indeed not done much noteworthy to give back to the industry.

God willing, it flashed in my mind that a need exists for sales professionals in building-material industry and I can serve the need by coming out with a tailored book that can help them cement their excellence. Numerous books exist on sales management, selling skills and a lot many factors associated with it. These are books on excelling in generic sales function or with a particular focus, such as on FMCG, consumer durables, pharmaceuticals, etc. In the context, this book has focused on achieving excellence in selling cement and other building materials.

I have considered some immortal truths and values of life that goes into the tasks of the job. This effort gives me confidence that the values taken up as imperative in the book will eventually help people to excel in all walks of life, without getting restricted to the sales function.

India, being the second largest cement producer in the world, has thousands of job opportunities, in the sales function of the industry. Moreover, India, as a developing economy, has a long period of profitable growth left for cement and building-material products, which means there are going to be lakhs of job openings in the sales function for cement and other building materials in the upcoming years. The same is the case with most of the other developing countries which have an excellent period of growth bound to come and stay longer.

To live up to the advice of the VC and answer my conscience, I endeavour to make this book help sales professionals achieve excellence in all walks of life and have a great career in cement and other products in building-material industry.

ABOUT THE AUTHOR

Dr. E Ravishankar, B.Sc., PGDM (S&M), MBA (Fin), M.Phil, MS, Ph.D. (M&A), is working as a business consultant in India's number one consulting firm for the cement industry.

He began his career as a pickle salesman and then for a decade had stints in selling FMCG, consumer durables, automotive and pharmaceutical products before embarking a career in the cement industry. In the cement industry for over two decades, he has served corporate giants in India, namely L&T, Aditya Birla and JSW.

He has written articles in India's leading national newspaper Economic Times; published case studies in international magazines and Indian journals. He has presented papers in sales, strategy and finance domains in several international and domestic conferences.

He did his MS and Doctorate from India's premier institute, Birla Institute of Technology and Science, Pilani.

Dr. Ravishankar hails from a middle-class family in the city of Chennai, India. Follows cricket as a pastime favourite. He loves kids Ms. Akshata and Ms. Tejaswi.

CONTENTS

INTRODUCTION

The objective of this book is to help sales professionals in building-material industry achieve stellar performance, establish a successful sales career, be top-notch leaders, and, apart from these, be excellent human beings, to lead a happy life.

Management guru Peter Drucker observed, for companies, "being good is not good enough", as competition has become intense. What the guru observed at the company level, to me now looks true at an individual level, as the competition is intense for staff both within and outside their organizations.

In the current industry background where branded building materials face the heat of competition, this book in all earnestness is written to help sales professionals ride over the competition and make a niche for themselves. The principles, steps, methods, and values enumerated envisage 360-degree coverage of the job to help practitioners achieve all-round capabilities, which will support them in both profession and life.

The book has three parts. The first part details the foundation needed for achieving excellence in function and as an individual. The second part takes up the process needed to establish stellar performance, both in numbers and values. The final part is dedicated to helping achieve greatness in leadership roles in the sales function and lead a happy life.

Brief of what to expect from the chapters:

Part I: Foundation for Excellence
Chapter 1: Addresses the issue of respecting brand equity and to never allow the mind to treat branded building-material products like a commodity.

Chapter 2: Helps sales professionals to know and appreciate the significance and importance of the sales function to the organization; be proud to be a part of it.

Chapter 3: Explains the market structure and its constituents; also brings out the need to have a market structure, with the steps involved in creating it.

Chapter 4: Some of the basic values and habits that help to sustain sales performance are brought out to form the foundation for achieving higher levels of success.

Part II: Achieving Professional Excellence

Chapter 5: Helps to understand, and appreciates the important segments and ways to manage the segments effectively.

Chapter 6: A four-pronged approach that helps to excel in 360 degrees of the sales function is delved with in detail.

Chapter 7: This chapter is to help appreciate and treat market issues as opportunities.

Chapter 8: Perspectives of pricing are dealt with as a separate chapter for the significance it has on so many aspects for an organization.

Part III: Leadership: Transcend to Greatness

Chapter 9: This chapter is dedicated to achieving greatness in the leadership role of the sales function founded on four non-negotiable qualities.

PART I

FOUNDATION FOR EXCELLENCE

CHAPTER 1

SHAKE OFF THE MYTH

OBJECTIVE:

- *To understand how a branded item is different from a commodity.*
- *How to handle our brands objectively when we are put under pressure to treat it akin to commodities.*

WHY TAKE A LOOK AT COMMODITIES

Manufacturers first aim to get the right product for their markets. Branding with imagination comes later. Higher the investment costs more will be the pressure to make a mark of the brand rolled out. Converting raw materials into finished products, such as cement and steel, involves heavy investments in the manufacturing process. Investments are done to get the right processed finished product and not base materials; for, such a right product enables a firm to get the expected returns.

After bringing out such a product to address a need in the market, company officials appreciate the value and importance of developing a healthy and popular brand. Problems emerge when external forces try their best to treat the branded products as commodities to extract benefits. It is here, the field staff, if less informed or not properly enlightened, can buckle on some occasions and start subconsciously treating their brand like a commodity. Finished products should not fall into the category of commodities. If this thought is not well entrenched, one is likely to feel adjusting price is the best way to garner volumes.

I strongly feel a peep into understanding "what is a commodity" and "why branded items should not fall in that category" will be of great help to sales professionals to handle their brands with a lot more responsibility.

COMMODITY AND ITS CHARACTERISTICS

Commodities are products in the market, which a consumer perceives to be fundamentally the same. The channel bridge between producer and consumer does but little to differentiate the products. Product differentiation for commodities is limited to the intermediaries' tendency to cluster products of nearly the same price as one category.

Unfortunately, some building materials such as cement which is not a commodity gets treated this way in the market. As a result, only a few popular brands are perceived to be superior by consumers. Given the market environment, this itself is an achievement by such popular brands.

One of the foremost challenges firms in the industry face is to first insulate sales force from any external pressure to view their brands as commodities. This myth has to be de-mystified internally within the organization. The sales force will do well to know how this perception came in the first place. Has it come down the line from top management or the market? It can be realised that it has always been from forces external, in the market.

WHAT IS A COMMODITY?

Webster's Dictionary defines a commodity as "a good or service whose wide availability typically leads to smaller profit margins and diminishes the importance of factors like a brand name other than price". Upon evaluating the definition of a commodity, one can see how far off one is from the company's objective, by way of assuming or accepting one's brand like a commodity.

A commodity is an economic good. Mostly, it is taken from mother earth and traded for a price. For example, in the cement industry, a commodity called limestone is un-earthed, processed, converted with the addition of other compounds into a finished product. This truth needs to get into the veins of sales staff when some channel in the market treats their cement brand wrongly as a commodity, to resist it with conviction.

It is worthy to note that even among the true commodities, there is a possibility that if the seller does not differentiate each product, the buyer will do the differentiation before buying. The buyer does this based on his need. For instance, a rice customer might well ask for a variety of rice cultivated in a particular region, based on his experience. Another example can be wheat flour sold in departmental stores. There might be several unbranded varieties kept, but the buyer, according to his needs, will give a name on his own, say, based on the colour of the flour or the source of its origin, and ask for it. By appreciating that true commodity product get differentiated by the consumers, the myth of commonality among the finished products gets de-mystified.

Let us see how the commodity structure exists in India.

The broad structure of commodity operations in India is as follows:

Commodity exchanges and spot markets are two verticals. Both these are under the commodities forwarding market. Forwarding market comes under the Department of Consumer Affairs.

Department of Consumer Affairs:
- First vertical: Forwarding Market & Exchange-based Market
- Second vertical: Spot Market

The commodity products are broadly classified under four categories: Agriculture, Energy, Base Metals and High-value Metals. There are both national and regional exchanges.

As we can see above, building products that are processed and finished in no way can be categorized as a commodity. Sales force should not be in line with any individual or group, when they face pressure to treat their brand like a commodity, as their objective is to extract the least price.

As said earlier, sometimes the intermediary channel does the differentiation of products by categories. The distribution channel tends to cluster products into groups and accommodate a price for the group and sell to customers. The producers, if clear that their product is differentiable to competing brands, have to be alert in not getting into the trap created by the categorization at the distribution level.

For finished valuable products, the inference is, a customer is likely to differentiate the product he buys and asks for it. Differentiation of products is inherent for most of the buyers. Differentiation of products happens at a micro-level with most consumers, and this has to be used fully by the manufacturing firms. When the differentiation of products based on some parameters is inherent at customer level even for direct commodities such as agriculture products, cement-like building material being a derived finished product after heavy-duty processing of limestone has to stand firm on the aspect of its product identification. This truth has to be ingrained and the culture must be inculcated to see the product as different from commodities, and that it does not deserve to be treated like a commodity.

After shaking off this myth, other brand promotion and marketing activities can be undertaken by a firm. Activities such as product positioning, pricing, sales promotions and setting up services are taken up to improve brand equity and get the deserving returns. Sales professionals must respect their brand names, their products and treat them at their respective position they deserve in the market.

The challenge comes when two or more products are comparable in product quality parameters. This is very much prevalent due to the current level of development in technology with many product features, and most of the characteristics are replicated with ease by many firms. In the context of such competition, the need is more to improve ourselves and the services to make a differentiation in the market.

CONCLUSION

Branded products by no stretch of the imagination are commodities. External forces that treat your brand like a commodity does it to extract price advantage at your company's cost. After huge investments, research and product development, a branded product is rolled out to earn the deserving returns. It is prudent to shake off the myth and fully accept that branded items are not commodities. When under pressure from any corner of the market to treat your brand like a commodity, you shall earnestly protect the envisaged position of your brand.

CHAPTER 2

SIGNIFICANCE OF SALES DEPARTMENT

OBJECTIVE:

- *To drive home the significance sales function has for organizations.*
- *How this realization is important for sales functionalities to know their value to their firm, which helps in working with great pride and responsibility.*

CASH IS THE LIFELINE

The end consumer and the intermediaries who feed them with the product are the source of cash for any company. Cash being the lifeline of any company, sales function which handles end consumer and distribution channel to bring in cash flows plays a significant role in any organization.

Sales force should know their importance to the firm, as it will help them work with zeal and pride. Considering the vital role they play for the development of the firm, no member of the sales team should carry any negative complex, of any sort, in comparison to staff of other departments. The efficiency of the sales department helps increase the company's earnings. Marketing function finds and creates customer leads; sales function converts the leads into cash. Thus, the activities of both marketing and sales departments have one common objective, that is, to bring in cash flows to the company.

Corporates invest in setting up mines, material sources, plants, inventories, manpower and other needs required for a business. For the investment of these, the source of money is equity funds plus the debt taken from lenders. Both the sources of funds carry cost which can be served only from profits. The starting point for profit

9

is revenue received from consumers. It is the sales department which takes the responsibility for volumes and revenues. Appreciating this flow of cause and effect must help all sales professionals know how important their function is to any organization.

Sales function helps top line

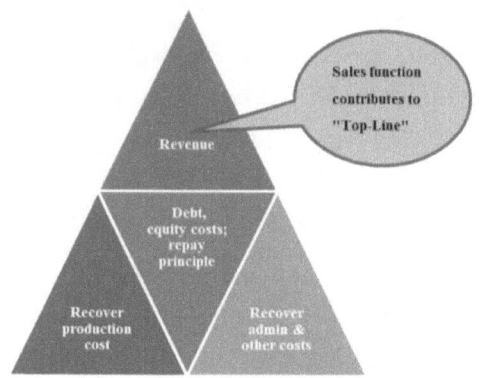

Figure 1: Revenue brought by sales function is the starting point for survival of an organization

Moreover, volumes and revenues achieved catch the attention of analysts and shareholders during quarter-end results. Sales volume gives an idea, if the company has probably gained, maintained or lost market share to competitors. The change in revenue gives an idea of changes in the top line of the business a company is in. Due to the dynamics of the capital market, it has become a culture across countries to give enormous importance to quarterly results as it has a bearing on the market capitalization of a company. Sales force efficiency, apart from bringing cash flows, has a direct bearing on the quarterly results of the firm, and hence, sales professionals stand to enjoy a high level of importance.

We can see sales force acting as the pillars for a firm. Be the maximum extent in quality; be as it ought to be, efficient and modern production methods; it is the sales department that needs to translate these positives, liquidate the produce and generate cash.

In many firms, sales function employees are paid handsome salaries vis-à-vis other departments due to the direct correlation the efficiency of sales force has with the top line of a firm.

CONCLUSION

Sales functionalities need to get into their internal system, the reality of their importance for the firm as generators of cash revenues, which is the top line for a firm. It is this cash that holds the key to recover production and administration costs, repay debts, serve debt and equity costs and to earn profit. This realization helps sales professionals to move with upright shoulders and show greater responsibility.

CHAPTER 3

MARKET STRUCTURE

OBJECTIVE:

- *To understand the importance of market structure and know its constituents.*
- *To realize that market structure forms the platform to achieve sales objectives.*
- *To delve on the steps to construct a market structure.*

CHANGING TIMES

Decades before, companies in building-material industry used to advertise in newspapers inviting the interested retail and wholesale entities for appointing as dealers for its products. They got an excellent response with numerous applications. They pruned and selected dealers to be the authorized outlets to sell their products. Today, if companies try this approach, the response will be anaemic.

Companies have to convince outlets of its utility and get acceptance. Excess capacity, multiple brands, market unpredictability, fluctuations in economic conditions all contribute to stiff competition. For this very reason, marketing thoughts gain more and more importance because finding a way out of the competition to create a unique identity for the brands is of greater relevance now. A medium is required to help establish the unique identity of a brand.

Creating and managing the intermediary channel consisting of retailers, wholesalers and influencers; finding and serving the end consumers directly or through intermediary channel are part of the core functions of the sales department.

The typical market structure for a building-material industry product is depicted in the chart form next.

The intermediary channel flow structure

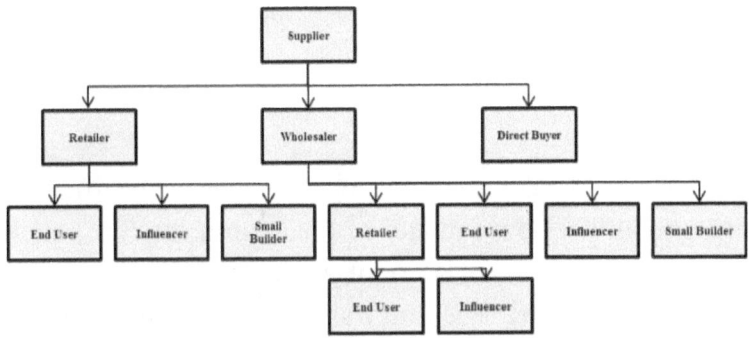

Figure 2: Typical market structure of a building-material product

SUPPLIER

Supplier refers to the firm creating and serving with the finished products. Taking the example of cement, manufacturers can have one or more production units of different types, which are as follows:

a) A fully integrated plant – where the basic raw materials such as limestone, laterite, bauxite and clay are extracted or procured and then processed to make the intermediate product that is called clinker. This clinker is then ground and mixed with 3 to 5% gypsum to make the finished product, called cement. The cement may be sold in loose or in packed form.

b) A grinding unit – where the intermediate product, clinker, is procured, ground and then mixed with 3 to 5% gypsum to produce cement.

c) A blending and packing unit – where cement in loose form is procured and then packed into bags.

d) Bulk terminals – where cement is stored in bulk and supplied in loose form.

The final product, cement, may be supplied to the trader or directly to the end-user or stored in warehouses and sold from the warehouse as and when required to the trader or end consumer.

All types of intermediaries have respective important roles in the building-material industry.

RETAILER

The retailer is the over the counter outlet for small scale contractors, influencers, and end or final consumer. The retailer is a trader who may trade a variety of products such as cement, steel along with other items. They may stick to one brand of a product variety or may have multiple brands. These retailers may take a product directly from a company or a bigger trader commonly referred as wholesaler. In rural towns, semi-urban and many urban cities, where construction of individual houses or repair work are widespread, these retail counters, form the backbone for selling building-material products for the suppliers.

WHOLESALER

They are bigger size traders who buy materials from the supplier and distribute it to the retail counters. They also sell directly to building contractors, bulk consumers and influencers.

DIRECT BUYER

Big-sized construction firms, institutions, commercial organizations, state-owned departments and building contractors involved in large construction projects buying in bulk quantities may like to have direct negotiation with the supplier to get price advantage. This mode of purchase is in vogue across countries.

END-USER

The end-user is the final consumer. From small repair works to big house constructions the final user may buy his building-material requirements from a retailer or wholesale merchants. When projects, as explained earlier, purchase building materials directly from a supplier, the buying firm is the end-user.

INFLUENCER

Any individual or group of individuals or a registered agency, recommending to consumers or decide the purchase of a product on behalf of customers, is an influencer for the product. For instance, in cement business influencers can be masons, civil engineers, building contractors and architects. For example, in individual house constructions, the house owner may take the advice of masons, contractors before buying materials or leave it to his civil engineer to decide on the brand(s) to be used.

SMALL SCALE BUILDER

These are building contractors, mostly civil engineers who undertake house and small scale commercial constructions; and such small sized projects.

CONSTRUCTING A MARKET STRUCTURE

As seen earlier, constructing a market structure is a primary requirement for sales professionals. Often the structure and its management prove to be running tap for the free flow of orders or to be the bottleneck inhibiting the free flow. Hence, a lot of mental energy needs to be exercised in deciding and constructing an efficient and appropriate market structure.

RESEARCH

Whether it is a new territory for an existing product, a new product for a new territory or if you are taking charge of a new territory, research of the market to see what intermediary channel is befitting for your product is necessary.

When a new territory is sought for an existing product, you need to figure out the existing structure for all the competing brands of your product type. Here you need to focus more on the brands which are likely to be benchmarked by you as an immediate competitor.

I would say give due regard to the market structure and its strength of the successful brand in the market, but for heaven's sake, do not conclude that is the best for your product in that market. In India, in the telecom sector, how a large corporate group pulverized the already set market with its new brand is an open case study.

I am not advocating the methods adopted in the telecom sector, but the point I derive is to figure out what is the gap that exists for customer satisfaction parameters in a market, and attacking the gap is more important than blindly following an existing leader. If you are convinced that the structure of the existing player is excellent for the market, then alone you may take it.

You need to figure out which part of the intermediary channel plays a major role for the market leader. Figure out if it is retail, wholesale, influencer or direct consumers. In other words, try and figure out, if it is predominantly B (Manufacturer) to retail; B to wholesale; B to wholesale to large consumers; B to influencers to large consumers; B to C (direct consumers) etc. Markets will be a combination of these, and you need to dig out what is predominant in that particular market.

If your product is new, the research will be even more interesting as you also need to estimate the acceptance level for the product type you are to propose for the market.

If you take charge of a new territory, where your brand already exists, the research must be to study your structure vis-à-vis other brands to know if your existing structure needs to be tweaked for betterment.

PLANNING

After understanding what market structure exists and is needed for your brand, you need to plan your activities to construct the right structure. In deciding what can be the best for a market, if you are a leader, it is worth seeing the pros and cons of all the permutation combinations possible keeping your team and then decide. When trying to brainstorm with your team the process must be to kick the ideas around and take feedback.

If a field officer has to make the study, he can give his data collected, inferences made and suggestions to his superior and then take up the planning. The planning must be to scheme and map which location, how many counters, if retail or wholesale and how many direct party agents are required to bring into the system. In case if the market is dominated by direct consumers, then the major direct buyers in the locality and the level of conversions required need to be planned with the schedule for achievements.

EXECUTING

Execution is the most challenging part which will render you a lot of lessons on the market and shape of things to come. In a way, it helps you to be well-prepared and be proactive when designing sales promotions, marketing activities and service requirements. In case if you are to build a retail-based system, then there is no substitute for leg work. See as many retailers as possible, do a lot of detailing, show records to reflect yours and your company's standards. While doing so, you need to minute the requirements of the retailers and make a record of sorts to deliver such requirements in the future to make a mark for yourself and your company.

In case of need to build a wholesale structure, I would prefer teamwork for the visits. Wholesale is a double-edged sword, in the sense of big volumes on one side and sensitive issues on the other side. The issues can be any one or more of credit needs, pricing needs, selling practices adopted, etc. A careful study of these is required, for not ending up with a cannibal effect of gobbling your own network, with the big trader shunning your prospects of network expansion.

CONTINUOUS MONITORING

Thus, we can infer from the above that market structure can have a make or break effect on sales flows. Its strength and versatility is so important, the market structure needs to be monitored for parameters such as: effectiveness, expansion, additions, substitutions, and, in rare cases, controls or deletions.

CONCLUSION

The market structure serves as the platform to enable the sale of your branded products. Research, planning, executing, continuous monitoring and restructuring are required to have the market structure in the right shape, strength, and flexibility to achieve the objectives.

CHAPTER 4

VALUES AND HABITS FOR SUSTAINED PERFORMANCE

OBJECTIVE:

- *To get into the two crucial values that help sustain sales performance.*
- *To understand the characteristics that need to be exercised and some habits that needs to be eschewed for successful sales performance across territories.*

THE TWO CORE VALUES

After seeing successful people in cement selling, consolidating their strengths and effective habits, I could garner two underlying simple truths. I share these with you, as I find they are simple and effective value-based tools, to help sustain sales performance.

VALUE THE NEED

A successful sales official shared this incident with me as to how it shaped his approach to dealers.

When this executive was in a dealer counter, a customer came asking for cement for his house construction. The dealer, a popular trader with many brands under his dealership, immediately started explaining a few brands at length and the prices. The customer had said in between that he wanted cement for his house project, which was to start anytime. But the dealer presented the brands he explained earlier and the prices and started asking for the location of dispatch, time, quantity etc. Not looking comfortable, the customer politely walked off without buying.

Two hours later the same official was in another counter. The same customer happened to walk into this counter too. This dealer was also popular but had less number of brands under his belt. This dealer enquired about the house size, style and requirements in the house and what made the customer construct a house in that place. The dealer listened to the customer's details and offered three combinations by way of value to the customer's needs. My friend executive silently observed as the dealer explained how the combination worked for the customer's benefit. The dealer politely briefed other requirements for the betterment of a house and how his counter may be of value for the same. Looking comfortable, the customer acceded and started placing the order with payment terms.

The official told me this shaped his approach by asking himself, "What was the difference between the two counters? Both are popular dealers, and the one who lost this sale had popular stocks in his yard. Why the customer chose the other dealer?"

The sales official said, after the incident, he maintained the habit of understanding the need of the customers and offering valuable suggestions to them. He decided to serve the customers and not try to sell to the customers. He wanted sales as an outcome of his service. This, he says, helped him to get the confidence and patronage of the dealer network for the rest of his career.

SERVE DON'T SELL

This event gives an important insight into the right attitude and approach for a salesman to have while handling a potential dealer. Don't sell looks like a negative statement, but here it means serving the network will get better sales than selling to the network without an attitude of serving them. Hard selling for volumes alone will give a selfish picture of the individual to the dealer community. Dealers already know an official has a job on hand to sell his products through his counter. After understanding the needs of a dealer fine-tune the strengths of the company to serve the needs and thereby bring up sales. Star performers had this trait in them. They served the network to earn volumes. The corollary is true too. Many professionals who did not keep an eye on serving the network met with failure. Once you serve you don't have to push hard for volumes. Rather, on occasions when the volume is required desperately to close a month on better levels, you can expect the network to be more cooperative.

Returning to the example, the second successful dealer in the event explained earlier, listened to understand the customer needs; added value to the customer over and above his expectations he originally had when coming to make the purchase. More importantly, this winning dealer did not try to sell a brand; rather, he tried to add value to the customer. He did not push across to the customer and start deciding on behalf of the customer. One has to allow the customer to decide after closing the sale. Taking decisions that the customer has to take will result in interfering with the liberty of the customer. The customer does not like to lose his freedom of decision-making. The same principle applies to retailers and wholesalers. They need to be served without affecting their freedom to think and decide.

When handling a direct customer, these steps hold good even more since it is unlikely that a sales executive will know the personal characteristics of a direct customer. The field force has to figure out the need and see how he can add value to the customer.

There is a principle in the game of cricket. When a batsman is to bat on a doubtful pitch, he has to play along the ground. The underlying meaning is batsman has to play the ball with extra care. By drawing an analogy, in the case of direct customers, since unknown aspects of the customers are likely to be high, one has to handle them more carefully.

Within the decision limits the sales official enjoys, what all he can do, to serve the dealers' needs, will have a huge bearing on good relationships and its results. The requirements can be many.

An official can be thorough with these only if he has an eye to understand the dealer. It needs to be remembered that the benefit that pertains to a dealer, or customer as the case may be, is limited to his needs. The rest is irrelevant to the dealer or the customer. Repeating parrot-like what is irrelevant to customers will create boredom for the customer. Hence, knowing the requirements of the customer and serving them becomes important.

Once a sales officer understands the customer requirements to get buttressed, it opens doors for further business expansion. Sales officials, once in a while, have to present to the dealer how he has served the dealer, as these kinds of small positive feedbacks can help to improve the counter share with the dealer.

CHARACTERISTICS TO REMEMBER IN FIELDWORK

Within a country like India (or between countries), multiple cultures and languages are involved. As companies are showing the hunger to operate in more than one region, field people may have to work in different regions and markets. For instance, after going through important markets in all the five zones of India, I found that there are characteristics common across regions. Knowing the habits field forces need to remember and exercise; what habits they can better avoid doing would help them be successful performers in any market.

HABITS TO EXERCISE

- *Face time with the customer*: Digitalization has been improving continuously. Some digital methods used five years back may get remodelled currently, and this trend may move on in future. At the end of the day, the time spent by the field force with the network has a huge bearing on results. Irrespective of the location, I found the dealer network values the sales official highly who visits them regularly. Knowing the stock level or requirements of a dealer over the phone should not be a deterrent to having more face time with him. Dealers tend to have a better respect for the company if the field force visits them regularly and spends quality time at the counter.

- *Customer belongs to company:* Appreciate the fact that all types of customers are company's assets and not yours. If you have to handle the physical assets of the company, such as Laptops, etc., carefully, you need to appreciate how much more care is needed to handle customers who are company's long-term assets. Dealers are the direct revenue generators and some dealers are non-replaceable. Whatever might be the approach and attitude of the customers towards you, as a sales professional you should refrain from taking things personally. There is no room for personal likes and dislikes for a sales professional to be applied to customers. This is the most fundamental attitude a field staff should inculcate in his mind.

- *Temperament is vital:* Even when a customer is tough and rude with you, the sales professional that you are must be stunningly calm and unaffected and be focused on solving the issue. If a customer is acquired after showing such excellence in temperament, apart from other good qualities, maybe the customer would remain acquainted for a long time into the future. This may even shut the doors for a competitor to take a share in the counter.

- *Mind the tongue:* Try being as diplomatic as possible and never hurt customers. Show as much humility and empathy to customers in words. It will do well in the long run, trust me, and it should come from within truthfully, and not by pretension.

- *Mind your body language:* As a sales official, you have experience in handling many types of customers, but mostly with the brands you might have been associated with. It needs

23

to be remembered that a dealer meets salespersons from different industries and maybe doing it for decades. The way a dealer reads a sales official might be more precise than how you as a sales official can read a dealer. Hence, a body language in line with what is communicated will be of immense value in getting into the good books of the customers.

HABITS TO ESCHEW

- *Sensitive issues:* Sensitive issues, involving politics, religion, caste, etc., are better to be avoided. Suppose if it is clear that the owner of a shop is skewed towards a particular political party, even then it would be better to avoid as some of his staff or life partner, who may be involved in the crucial aspects of the business, maybe otherwise. As said earlier, customers are company's asset; anything which can damage them should be shunned.

- *Speaking of negativities of the customer*: Dealers would have both positive and negative characteristics. Our business is to use the positives by encouragement. Negatives, if any, that needs to be changed constructively, can be an outcome of a productive discussion. But, we should not harp on the negatives, which is an important aspect for us to remember. I take this point, as I have seen many field officials commit this mistake, say, in the midst of a tense discussion. As simple example: if a counter has lower sales volumes vis-à-vis other counters in the location, efforts might be only to encourage the growth of the business without hurting the counter's lower standing in the market by way of volumes.

- *Speaking ill of your staff:* Never talk ill of a colleague or superiors to a customer. It might be temporarily engaging, but in the long run, it will only cause problems for you. Company colleagues and superiors are a part of your company's army.

While the dealer is not an enemy, capturing the market is an objective of the army called "sales team"; and all team members are engaged with that objective. Never let down a colleague or spread ill will. When things get to the ears of the colleague, it will have a severe bearing on the teamwork. Sometime into the future, a colleague might be your boss or a direct report or in a department of need to you. In any of these cases, bridging the gap created due to spreading ill will would be a herculean task and might well make it a problem for you and the company.

- *Speaking ill of industry colleague:* Never make negative personal remarks of an industry colleague to the dealer or end consumer. Though there can be provocative situations arising, it is required on your part to restrain yourself. Such restraint is an investment you are making for the future and not a loss, as you might imagine at that moment. Restraining oneself is a greater strength than letting oneself **rudderless**. The business world is small: you may have to move closely with the very person you deride, at some point of time in the future, which is not under your control.

CONCLUSION

Digging in to know the needs of intermediaries and serving them are the two core values that help achieve positive sales results and sustain them in the long run. As movers across regions and territories for career growth, the habits to exercise in the field and the habits one is better off without are to be applied manfully.

PART II
ACHIEVING PROFESSIONAL EXCELLENCE

CHAPTER 5

SEGMENT CARE

OBJECTIVE:

- *To understand the significance of retailers, wholesalers and direct consumers.*
- *To dig into productive ways of managing them with care.*
- *To appreciate how the principle of empathy can be put into action.*

RETAIL MANAGEMENT

Before going into how we can take care of retailers, I feel describing the roles of retailers and what is their significance is important.

Retailers and their significance

In simple terms, a retailer satisfies the need for a final or end consumer, who purchases the product for consumption. In other words, the purchase is not for trading, rather for consumption. I believe any entity that supplies to end-user is doing a retailing act. The idea of direct supply to a final customer has usurped in many industries including building materials. In the long run, in developing economies particularly, it has been the role of the retail outlets to do this function, in building material industry.

Retail counters satisfy some major requirements of manufacturers.

They can be summarized as follows:

- ***Reach:*** The product has to reach remote corners of the market to make use of the awareness of the brand, and or need of the product. For some products, that requires to be stored and propagated in the locality, retail counters become the best option. If customers need small quantities with minimum fuss and maximum ease, the availability of retail counters satisfies the requirement.

- **Peters down risk:** Risk can be with respect to a product, its storage and the associated financial aspects. To hold stocks of perishable products say like cement, a retail counter comes as a ready solution as they know the movement levels and store accordingly. Knowledge of demand of the location is required for optimum storage, which retail counters can do adeptly. Product risk comes by way of theft, damage etc., which gets mitigated as a retailer once purchases a product, absorbs this risk. Selling to end consumer needs flexibility in credit and its related transaction adjustments, for which retail counter is more suited to carry out the function.

- **Ease of business:** After selecting a product for the first time for house construction, the future purchase can be conveniently done even over the phone, depending on the relationship between a retailer and the customer. Unlike, say like clothing items, physical presence and comparisons are not mandatory for building materials during every time of purchase.

- **Enjoys an emotional link:** For an end-consumer, emotional quotient in selecting a particular building material does not play a great role, unlike, say for food, clothing products or consumer durables such as automobiles. The final user is more likely to be rational and risk-averse; value the price against these parameters rather than getting locked with a product emotionally. The emotional aspect might come into play in selecting the retailer who gives excellent advice and support services, which reflect the importance of the retailer in the selling structure.

- **Handles a variety of customers:** End consumers, particularly if they decide to buy the product directly from retail counters, are bound to vary widely. A retailer can do the detailing for the consumer and serve his need with the right product. One customer may be price-conscious; others may be focused on safety aspects etc. For the construction work undertaken by the end consumer, shortlisting the products for the first time are very crucial and needs some close detailing. For this purpose, a popular retail counter having a good reputation in a location becomes useful for an end consumer. After deciding the products, the future purchases can be managed even over telephonic conversation. The range, vastness, depth, and variety of customers cannot be reached by manufacturers or by wholesalers directly as served by the retail outlets available locally. This in a way can be referred to as the most comprehensive service a retailer does to the industry, which is pertinent in developing economies where awareness is less and every penny counts for the public due to economic conditions.

- *Connectivity:* Retailers' connections with influencers such as masons, building contractors also make it almost mandatory requirement for the manufacturers to maximise their retail base. This is the best tool to achieve market penetration to achieve volumes. To satisfy different types of customers in a locality, the retailer becomes the "go to" intermediary for manufacturers.

- *Flexibility and modifications:* Based on the customer needs of a locality, some retailers modify their services.

  - A retailer may have one product and one brand popular in the area and serve the market.

  - Another type may have one product category but a range of brands to serve various needs for that product category – say steel, cement, paint, etc.

- A retailer may have multiple brands in different product categories such as cement; paint etc., and serve a wide range of customers.

- **Retailers as influencers:** Retailers who have a high local standing are likely to be very powerful influencers. If they have gained a reputation by giving quality products coupled with an unbiased approach to customers, the end consumer is highly likely to go to them to take advice on what materials to use for his construction work. It is easier for a retailer to build confidence with an end consumer than what an advertisement can do for a product. When a retailer having a reputation for serving the right products recommends a product to an end consumer, then any level of promotion from a manufacturer to that customer contrary to the advice is unlikely to have an impact with the customer.

In this context I like to share a personal experience of how retailers' feedback changed my life, for the better:

When I was working in a profit-making public sector firm, of Government of India, I got selected for a job in one of India's biggest corporate names, Larsen & Toubro Ltd. (L&T), for their cement sales division. Leaving a public sector job is something not even considered by many in India, and I had to take a tough decision. Also, my entire family was against me leaving a secured job. I went and did a little survey meeting four reputed retail counters to get inputs on L&T's cement brand. All four retailers delivered a unanimous message to me: With L&T they take the product confidently, as customers accept it with full conviction and find their collections also easy. For dealing with that brand the retailers' only consideration with the company was their margins, which suffered due to the competition. They felt all other aspects associated with the product were top class. They also conveyed the people who addressed them from the company were top drawer stuff. After getting this message, same day from that location itself, I went to a photo-copier shop and faxed my resignation to my company; sent an acceptance letter of the job offer to L&T. Ever since, I am attached to cement industry. Such can be the power of reputed retailer's words.

- *Build brand equity:* If a brand is available in many counters, the end consumer is likely to get enormous faith in the brand and see it as a value product to rely upon. To have brand displayed in many retail counters coupled with advertisement campaigns can give an enormous boost to the image of the brand. A customer is likely to think "If a product is available in many places, it indicates many people use this and it has to be good". Once this perception enters a consumer's mind, the price of the brand will be seen as value-based, which will result in reduced number of consumers who negotiate heavily on its price.

- *Manufacturers' profitability:* More retail counters as dealers mean the distribution is widespread. This results in the average sale quantity per counter for a brand to come down, as the sale made by a few counters is replaced by many counters. This reduces the outgo of "volume-per-dealer"-based incentives, which is a saving for the company.

Continuous monitoring and restructuring

In a decade or thereabouts, the need to continuously monitor and restructure the retail network has become important for brands. Due to the increase in competition, waning margins, increase in the cost of running retail outlets, improved global connectivity, better education standards which makes progeny of retailers to take different professions and for various other reasons which go with improving economies, the number of retail outlets which close down operations, and the new ones entering the fray are increasing.

This makes, continuous restructuring of the network very crucial for sustaining sales volumes. Having retailers at vantage locations is a huge support system for manufacturers to achieve customer reach.

Care power

"There is nothing more energizing to oneself than exercising love to fellow beings", goes an old Sanskrit teaching.

One of the ways of expressing love is to take care of others we are involved with. Apart from our act of helping others, it helps us in the end, by way of energizing us and making us feel contented with our acts. As success breeds success, the effects of such fruitful acts grow in geometric proportions. You, as sales professional, to achieve excellence need to take care of direct reports, distribution channel partners, direct customers and Influencers. In the competitive environment, I would say apart from these, you have to embrace competitors also and have healthy relations. Excellence will be reflected in the long run.

Developing retailers with care

One of the best ways to take care of a retailer is the requirement to lend support for his retail sales. In most countries, retail is run as a proprietary business with owners having direct contact with consumers. If sales officials can address their (retailer's) consumers and satisfy them, it can work wonders for building the relationship and loyalty of the retailer. If a sales official at ground level can do this, it will be the difference between "performer" and "also ran" in the market.

To do this, one must have a desire of the heart to take care of the retailer, the brand he is selling and the end-user who makes the company survive. When a retail owner gets the confidence that a company official addresses his cash cows (that is, the end consumer), his image of the company will change for the better.

The good culture of the sales team of the company which handles the territory will get established in the market. The connectivity between the retailer and the field official will become wonderfully bonded. I find most of the companies work up to the retail level. Very few successful ones step further and reach the end consumer, and brands of such firms' command recall in the market.

Companies need to get their field officials to meet the retailers, spend time with him and get sales volumes. Based on the importance and size of the market, companies have the manpower deployed in the areas. A company, in markets classified as important for that firm, if develops this culture of going up to the end consumer to meet him and address requirements will have a huge advantage over firms which come from distant locations to dump volumes at lower prices to improve plant capacity utilizations.

Instead of suffering at the hands of lower priced brands one way a popular and well-placed brand in its important market can hold its retailers is by being close to the retailer's end consumers. Philip Kotler observes emotions have a strong influence on purchase and brand support decisions. This view suggests the emotion factor has a high correlation with sales outcomes. By giving excellent after-sales service to retailers, their emotional needs can be captured. For instance, by trying to be close to the consumers who have purchased cement from retail counters, a company in effect is inducing the end consumer to make repeat purchases which will help the concerned retailer. This makes the retailer even happier, encouraging him to take initiative to sell the brand resulting in additional volumes.

Taking cement industry, for example, some of the requirements end consumers can aspire for can be listed as follows:

- To know how important cement is for his building.

- What care he must take during the construction period.

- Timely delivery of the right volumes.

- Coordination with the retailers who caters to him.

- Any schemes which company runs to incentivize end consumers.

- How the end consumer saves with the brand.

- Give some encouraging points of the retailer who caters to him and leave some brochures etc. with the end consumer to give him full confidence.

- Above everything, the end consumer needs to have a "feel-good" factor, for his purchase decision.

It is observed that individual house constructions are done by giving contracts that fall into three broad categories:

- An individual may contract a total rate for his house, after deciding the size and design – which includes the cost of material, labour, professional charges and margin of the builder.

- An individual may undertake the responsibility to purchase the materials and have a construction contract.

- An individual may absorb the cost of buying construction material, as and when it is incurred, but gives the responsibility to the builder to procure them and fixes an amount for construction work.

In many cases, it has been observed that masons have a say on the purchase of the materials. If the company's field official develops a culture of addressing the end consumer, then the knowledge of what influenced the purchase decisions of the end consumer will give an excellent platform for building sales and marketing programs for the location. If most of the purchases are done by the end consumer, the schemes can be packed to address end consumers; if it is predominantly masons then mason-focused schemes can be made more popular; if it happens to be the builders, then sales-promotional programs need to be tuned towards them.

In some cases, making a retailer reveal their buyers details can be a challenge, as some retailers may not like the company to know the details. Here, the confidence that the field official gives to the retailer to help him sell easily and make his name more popular in the area will be of enormous help. After retailers witness the good actions of the field officials, they will be forthcoming to share details. The success with few retailers can make other retailers who were apprehensive to open up. A company, with enough manpower to address retailers this way, can enjoy a huge advantage over competitors who cannot have adequate manpower.

There is a powerful factor that attracts retailers

Retailers love brands that sell easily, which customers like consuming and don't complain. This is simple to understand because it saves huge effort and time for the retailer and also helps him get his collections better. In such cases, a retailer prefers to buy against cash, makes a quick sale and covers a larger canvas to increase his customer base and income. With a well-accepted brand, you actually serve a retailer better.

Other important things that a retailer may be happy to be taken care of are:

- Getting his orders catered as per need.
- Sales personnel giving him a proper listening to his needs.
- Promises put into action.

- Spending enough face time with the retailer and befriending him.

- Having knowledge of his family structure and giving timely wishes and greetings, giving a token of appreciation of the achievements of his children.

All these put together can help to get a grip of retailers' emotional needs and satisfying it. Due to the small size of the entity, it is easier to work on the emotional needs of a retailer and build the relationship.

WHOLESALER MANAGEMENT

Significance of wholesaler

Retailers and trading agents, for their business, buy material from larger trading houses called wholesalers. Wholesalers are mostly larger business entities than a retail shop keeper. The wholesalers' main weapon is their contacts to get business. Financially sound a wholesaler may be, but without business contacts he will come a cropper sooner or later.

Wholesalers render their service in many ways

Cash sales wholesalers

This type of trader deals mostly on cash sales to other traders keeping a thin margin. This type of trader prefers to deal with popular, fast-moving brands. They make a profit on volumes got from a large customer base and repeat purchases. There is a band of retail outlets that prefer this type of trader to approach as it helps them enjoy good margins in spite of not buying directly from manufacturers. If a product is fast moving and retailer can afford the cash purchase and if the retailer feels confident of re-selling in cash to the end-user, this type of wholesaler comes in handy. There will be a lot of occasions when a retailer wants small volumes, repeatedly, and is willing to buy against cash. These retailers invariably have a good set of customers who buy in cash and become very important for manufacturers. For the timing, frequency and small purchase quantity per invoice, manufacturers cannot cater to them directly and hence this type of wholesaler becomes the stronghold to cater to this section of retailers to squeeze extra volumes.

It is good to remember that if a brand sells against cash; its brand equity will surge ahead in the mind of all the parties involved in the purchase transaction. If a good brand has to improve its brand equity further, it must encourage cash sales in retail and wherever possible in wholesale.

This type of wholesaler holds inventory or relishes a company arranged warehouse available locally, as timely, quick supply is the essence of his business model. If supplies are intermittent, his entire business model will collapse. These wholesalers help manufacturers achieve higher sales volumes when they happen to run any special sales-promotional schemes which are volume-based to push volumes.

Agent wholesaler

This type of wholesaler does not hold stocks but acts as a link between buyer and manufacturer facilitating the purchase. In building materials, if the buyer happens to be a direct consumer with a decent volume at stake, these wholesalers may try to get involved or coordinate closely with manufacturers to decide the price of the transaction. If the buyer happens to be a retailer, it is invariably on some pre-agreed terms between the agent and the buyer. These agents agree for commissions for sales billed directly to end-user or undertake to invoice on their entity and absorb the responsibility for payment.

As the economy grows, purchases in large quantities are likely to increase across corners in the cities and towns. Having contacts with all the pockets from where demand emanates is not practically feasible for manufacturers, and hence, these agent wholesalers might play an important role in the future for realizing this demand.

Comprehensive wholesalers

These types of wholesalers are the "go-to" entities for manufacturers to achieve reach and volumes. If manufacturers have to achieve this level of reach directly, the exercise may prove to be very costly.

A comprehensive wholesaler will have a full-fledged team: sales force, key accounts caretakers, finance & accounting experts, warehouses, logistics and possibly e-commerce service too. Their customer range is huge by way of size, variety and geographical spread. In the building materials industry, some wholesalers run business for multiple generations, though this trend is waning now.

Their main business comes through serving retail counters. These wholesalers scan and scout for retail counters who have requirements that cannot be satisfied by a manufacturer directly. For example, retailers who take small volumes and need credit cannot aspire to buy from manufacturers due to which these wholesalers who offer full service become the main source. In developing economies, retailers who do not have deep pockets will be large in numbers, and hence, comprehensive wholesalers are needed to feed the need and get volumes.

Apart from the above-described positives, additional advantages that wholesalers offer can be enumerated as follows:

- For manufacturers, market inputs acquired from wholesalers will be very broad and deep. The insight wholesalers have on the market will be very fine and precise knowing which can help manufacturers take the right decisions.

- All small retailers will not have transportation facilities but may require small delivery quantities free of cost, which a wholesaler can arrange as a part of his business process.

- A wholesaler takes care of the financial risk of small retailers.

- A local retailer, without much exposure, is more likely to believe a wholesaler he knows closely for business transactions and for dealing with a brand than the manufacturer directly.

- If by advertisement alone a manufacturer hopes to ensure his product is available well penetrated in the market, the expenses can be prohibitively high. A wholesaler who has business links will make it as easy as anything with little extra cost.

- When the market has different types of requirements, a wholesaler would have done the homework and be ready with serving the needs. A manufacturer will take a long time to get into the finesse of the market, if at all he succeeds in this venture, in all the markets.

- Wholesalers save manufacturers in moments of crisis for achieving volumes, as they can absorb volumes taking initiatives with their clients.

- In the absence of wholesalers, if the manufacturer decides to serve all pockets with short delivery time, the warehouses' cost will be substantially high and non-maintainable.

Developing wholesalers with care

In the competitive environment, care is a need, as it should be, as a basic requirement for success in sales performance. Care is to treat a trader as a member of your company.

Care of wholesaler is required from two perspectives: one is to care for his business entity, and another dealer's emotional side.

Due to the relatively larger size of a wholesale counter, extra care is to be applied to the business needs, as errors can prove to be very costly for both the wholesaler and your company. The fact that the survival of a wholesaler also depends on the administration and management skills of his enterprise makes serving his business needs very important. The business requirements can range, from a simple supply instruction to help him solve a complex issue of say solving his outstanding dues. Care can range from a simple everyday telecom conversation, to being ready to be in his spot to address critical issues affecting the trader.

The common service area where a wholesaler understands he is taken care of is to listen to his requirements sincerely and addressing it. For example, his requirements can be related to price clarity, availability of materials, helping him use his fleet, protecting his retail network, helping him build a retail network, increase direct purchasing customer base, the supply of fresh materials, supply in time and logistics coordination.

TAKING CARE OF "DIRECT PARTIES"

Direct customers may be handled directly by a company official or through agents who mobilize and bring business from direct consumers.

With greater urbanization, a higher percentage of sales volumes are to be achieved from direct parties every succeeding year. The percentage share of direct parties in total sales volumes is likely to increase. This makes the need to focus on his segment more on a micro-level for companies. Even in markets regarded as tertiary by a firm, catering to the direct parties has become a need. For example, urban cities have the scope of consuming high volumes.

In cement business, for instance, a firm that has its factory located at far off location from an important city may have to serve it to achieve volumes. Any volume possible at prices over and above the variable costs helps reduce fixed cost per unit; any volume achieved at realizations over and above the fixed cost and variable cost contributes positively to the EBITDA. Hence, many urban areas, which can consume volumes, can be attractive based on price levels. Very few exceptions, such as firms with high capacity utilization with limitation on brownfield expansions alone, can stand firm on having to focus only on-trade segment. Firms that strive for capacity utilization and serve urban and semi-urban markets have to cater to bulk consumers.

Care for direct parties can be: Proper and professional documentation, following business protocol, dealing with top officials at board level or at senior management level, handling influencers, help people who actually use the material at site, clarity in billing, adhering to product specifications, extending technical support, coordination for supplies and having a personal touch with people who matter for transactions.

Adhering to care on the essential elements specified above becomes rather crucial in the age of competition. When the price is more or less equal between brands, the aspect of care rendered will win volumes in the long run. This means care should not be ignored and left to the responsibility of the intermediary agent or trader.

VALUE OF EMPATHY

I strongly believe empathy derives from compassion. If one needs to be among the top 10% of the sales professionals, one need to have this factor of empathy embedded in his dealing with customers. Smaller the entity like a retailer, where the decision-making is from the owner, greater will be the return for empathy shown in dealings. Moreover, the aspect of empathy in handling trade parties will improve the name of the field professional in the market he operates. An improved brand equity one earns out of discipline shown in his dealings with empathy will save the professional in tough times. By tough times, I mean month-end sales pressure.

The objective of this book is to help sales professionals excel in their careers, not just be good performers. I dare say empathy in handling clients is as much-needed a factor as anything else maybe if one has to excel in his career.

The foremost habit you should develop in showing empathy is "Listening". Due to factors, such as sales pressure, continuous phone calls in the age of mobile phones, we are fast missing the art of listening face to face. Our luck would be such when we have to listen to a customer, a mobile call will invite our response, WhatsApp messages will drop in, etc. We need to keep these distractions off, make a conscious decision not to attend mobile calls when we listen to a customer. When the customer notices that we don't attend calls and listen to him, his confidence in us is likely to improve. Some sales professionals due to an ideology that they must be good in communication tend to confuse themselves thinking they need to do all the talking. When a customer speaks, whether it is a general dialogue or a sensitive one involving some issue to be resolved, as true sales professional, one has to listen to the customer without distractions. You may take down notes of the needs of the customer when he speaks which helps the customer gain faith in you.

While listening to the needs of the customer, we have to think like a customer to understand his requirements precisely. Empathy put into action is to act on the need of the customer after listening to him and understanding his needs. No lip service will work. This aspect also will differentiate a good salesperson from the masses because listening, noting down the needs of the customer, acting on the needs and serving him properly are disciplines most people falter at.

If we take our own experience in purchasing many things in life, we can acknowledge how happy and comfortable we were when the salesperson delivered as per the requirements expected for the purchase. We should have the attitude of delighting the customer with innovative actions and by going that extra mile to serve the customer.

To possess an attitude in understanding the basic needs that are to be satisfied, something that the customer legitimately requires, and then ensuring the customer gets those with proper coordination, is empathy put into action.

When you go to appoint a dealer, if the counter understands, as a sales official and as a company, you deal with empathy, then you stand a better chance to get acceptance of your dealership offer from that counter. If we micro-analyse the needs of a trader, it breaks down to three needs:

1. What the end customer wants to buy: The dealer would desire to serve his customers by making what they need available at his counter.

2. From which counter the end consumer wants to buy: The dealer would like his counter to be the one of choice for his customers.

3. At what value the end consumer is willing to buy: The dealer would want the customers to buy from his outlet considering it as the one delivering better value.

I used the word "value" instead of "price" here. There is a subtle yet substantial difference between these two words. *Price* means the price at which the product is sold. *Value* is the package of benefits the end consumer gets from the product for which he pays a certain amount convincingly.

If you prune down the needs of a dealer it will fall invariably into one of the above three factors.

If one refers to seven habits of highly effective people, of Covey, two of the seven habits are "to begin with the end in mind" and "think win-win". If the above three are catered to for the trader, it helps both the trader and the sales professional. Enabling the dealer to achieve the above-referred objectives, help the sales professional to strike a win-win chord with him. If the sales professional addresses these needs of the dealer, there is a high probability of a successful relationship sustaining with the dealer. If the trader is effective, he is going to give business in return, which is the objective of sales professionals. When both the trader and the sales professional are benefited, it is a win-win equation which helps to build a long-term relation with the dealer for the sales professional and the brand associated with.

When it comes to direct parties, it becomes the respect a field person has for the specific needs of the party. As long as the need is legitimate, having a genuine interest in serving it by making sincere efforts to satisfy them is empathy put into action. But the challenge is to get to know what the needs of the customer are. For that, the field force has to exhibit listening, understanding with proper questioning and thinking from the customer's point of view. If one puts oneself into the shoes of the customer, proper questions will come. But as a general rule for serving direct parties, a questionnaire prepared in advance on a pre-formatted form based on the experience will be immensely helpful.

Even if the end consumer or retail trader is not currently dealing with the brand or not giving first preference to your brand, if you meet him and spend quality time showing empathy, in case of any gap developing between the customer and a competitive brand he is dealing with, you stand a good chance of becoming an alternate choice.

Showing empathy is a standout characteristic. This is easy to say but difficult to practice. As sales professional, if you take this seriously and get it into your DNA and make it run in your veins; almost making it your second nature, you would stand out among the crowd of sales professionals operating in the region.

The thin borderline of empathy: As sales professional, you need to know the difference between empathy and sympathy as there is a subtle difference. *Sympathy* is to sympathize with the client and give him things to the level of sacrificing, whereas *Empathy* is to understand the point of view of the client putting oneself in the shoes of the client, then see the legitimate possibility of the firm and balance the needs. When empathy is put into action, one understands the client but need not agree with the client.

The advantage of having empathy over not having it is: In case of disagreement, a field person with empathy can explain the disagreement to the client appropriately without wounding him or creating division.

If empathy is crossed over towards sympathy, a salesperson may end up serving the client at the cost of a company's objectives. Hence, empathy is very important, but the borderline is thin and one should not cross over to the side of sympathy.

CONCLUSION

Appropriate care exercised on the market segments relentlessly benefits all those involved – the client, the sales professional and the firm. Empathy rendered in the interactions with customers and intermediaries makes for smoothness in the relationship. This also makes way for long-term relationships and consistent performance.

CHAPTER 6

THE FOUR PRONGED APPROACH

OBJECTIVE:

- *After deep dive into the foundation required for excellence, we get into the important aspect of the approach. With this approach, the endeavour is to achieve excellence in 360 degrees of work function.*
- *To delve into the subtle values embedded in the process that acts as a root for perpetuating great personality and performance.*

ALL ARE BLESSED

I strongly believe, to achieve success in the sales profession, it is not that some are born for it and others are not. In other words, if one applies himself properly with the right attitude, all can be successful in the sales profession. Whether we know or not, acknowledge it or not, somewhere we exhibit selling skills in our lives. All are blessed with selling skills, and to hone it further depends on our will.

KNOWLEDGE, DEVOTION AND APPLICATION, IS THE WAY FORWARD:

Swami Vivekananda insisted on education that doesn't just teach subject knowledge but develops one's personality as well in the process. The sales function is such a platform one should not end up being excellent in just achieving targeted numbers, rather, in the process one should transpire into a great personality, apart from the knowledge of his functions, in order to remain a great performer.

Bolstered with Knowledge, Devotion and Application (KDA), anyone can become a great asset to the company one is working for. When developed by a professional, it will be very hard for average performers in the market to match as they have to overhaul themselves.

This is my strong conviction: Take any great performers, we can find these three – knowledge, devotion and application – embedded in their performance. There would be a high level of devotion to things undertaken; knowledge required would have been acquired and applied. The sales profession is a wonderful platform to exercise devotion, knowledge and application by adopting a four-pronged approach, we shall delve in this chapter. Before going to the four-pronged approach, I consider it apt to describe why we all can acquire these three strengths. If we are convinced with ourselves that we can have it, how to go forward with these three can be understood in greater depth with ease. Before going with the approach for success, let me bring out how to frame ourselves.

KNOWLEDGE

"Knowledge" is the goal of man! Development of knowledge plays a key role in making a difference between evolution and stagnation. All of us can gain knowledge. The ability to gain knowledge is not a talent, for one to think some people have it whereas others are not blessed with it. Any normal person can be better off every year with experience, which means he gained knowledge. Once a hot vessel burns us, we don't touch it again. This is a simple case of knowledge applied from experience. The ability to acquire knowledge is inherent in man. The difference between knowledge and ignorance is one's chosen field is more to do with the efforts put in. Simple way of gaining knowledge is to exercise the question "why?", when you don't understand something. Everyone cannot know everything, but everyone can know more than what he already knew by making efforts. To me, a performing sales professional needs to have a quest for knowledge.

DEVOTION

All of us are devoted. Devotion is also inherent in man. A lazy person is devoted to laziness. If devoted to protecting our beloved ones, we protect them come what may in life. I have read a case of a village lady in her twenties managing to protect her 18 months old baby from the jaws of a leopard, which shows her devotion to save her kid. All of us are devoted to something or other. The thing is we don't realize it.

Repeated self-appraisal, by way of asking oneself "I am devoted to what?" channelizes a person. In the sales profession, devotion to objectives on hand keeps a person on track. That is to say, the devotion to other things which may dilute one from achieving his objectives must be less in intensity to the devotion one has to achieve his objectives. We see people casually say, they were not devoted to certain kind of job on hand and hence could not do it. By going one step further, when failure comes, one can realize one was devoted to something else which prevented one from being devoted to the job on hand. Devotion to something else swayed a person from his adopted course.

In other words, all of us have the capability to be devoted; the need is to regulate ourselves. Once the sales professional realizes this and gathers himself to be devoted to the right things he should be on the right track for excellence in the sales profession.

APPLICATION

The intention to apply oneself to a job on hand is under one's control. The degree to which one applies oneself depends on the liking one has to the action. The result of action can have many factors strung to it, but deciding to apply, to put his shoulders to the wheel, as it were, and hard work completely depends on the will of the individual. If we decide to undertake an action, but keep on postponing it at the slightest distraction, we can infer to ourselves that we have a dislike for the action. Succumbing meekly to likes and dislikes is a weakness. Then, to help put ourselves back on track, we need to introspect why we have a dislike, and is it justified to have such a dislike to do our duty.

From the clarity that devotion, knowledge and application can be achieved by all of us, we shall proceed to delve on how the four-pronged approach can help a professional excel in sales.

APPROACH TO THE SALES PROFESSION CAN BE BROADLY PUT INTO FOUR DIMENSIONS

The Four-Pronged approach

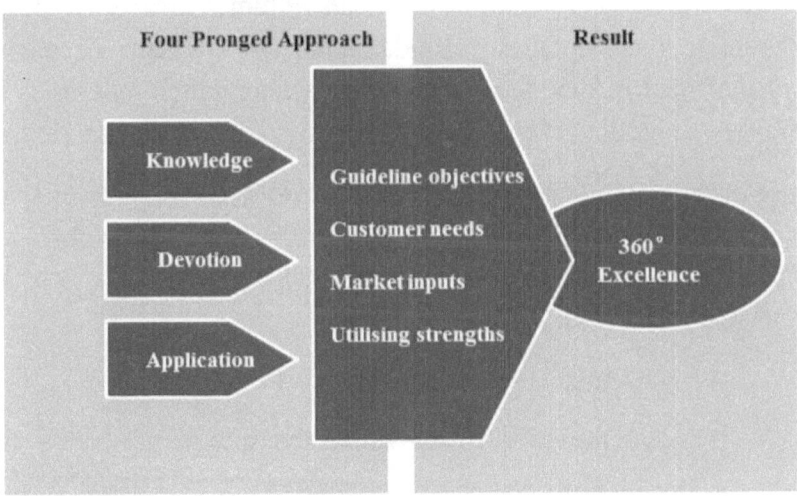

Figure 3: The Four-Pronged Approach for 360° excellence as sales professional

1. **KDA to Guideline Objectives**

2. **KDA to Serving Customer Needs**

3. KDA to Extracting Market Inputs

4. KDA to Utilizing Internal Strengths

1. KDA to Guideline Objectives

Shocking, but true, that knowledge of guideline objectives of a firm does not spread among all the employees in many firms. Even if known, only a few are devoted to the objectives. When these two are missing, constructive actions towards achieving the objectives does not transpire. It is important to remember that all of us take up a job after management selects us, which carries the message that if not for the selection we would not be in that job in the first place. That is, every penny earned from a job is because the management recruited us. To know and be devoted to the principles and objectives of the organization is mandatory. If the primary objective of the organization is to sell volumes profitably, being devoted to this becomes a fundamental requirement. There are some soft factors also to uphold which are unwritten, but holds as well, like upholding the name of the organization in the market.

The major guideline objectives, given by organizations to sales professionals are: to improve sales revenue, cash flow and profitability, albeit all these done with ethics. This can be translated as follows:

a. Revenue: Through volumes.

b. Cash flow: Collection within the time frame.

c. Profitability: Selling at the right price with the cost of distribution kept at optimum levels.

d. Following and upholding the company's rules, regulations, ethics and image.

1.1 Volumes

Volumes play a huge role in the business which involves high investment, large capacity, and demanding full capacity utilisations. When revenue increase is the agenda, the first thought that enters our mind is the need for higher sales volumes. But there are more subtle factors that make achieving high volumes important, not just the revenue factor. For instance, if we take the example of cement, it is high-volume, low-value, high-investment, perishable-branded product. Let us see some factors that make sales volumes important.

1.1.1 Helps reduce fixed cost: Higher volumes help reduce fixed cost per unit of production. When the production against capacity is at a low level, say less than 60%, the effect of improved volumes reducing the fixed cost per unit can be higher. While the fixed cost will vary for firms depending on its size and structure, higher volumes help reduce fixed cost per unit.

1.1.2 Catches investors' eye: The investors have become very obsessed with volumes achieved by the firms they have invested money. This can be referred from the way analysts assiduously bring to light any changes in volumes during their presentations of quarterly results.

1.1.3 Product used builds brand equity: When a product forms an important part of a project, such as cement in a house project, people give a lot of importance for the product used in the neighbourhood. More than advertisements and sales promotions, a product used by another customer gives much higher confidence for the buyer to buy a product, provided the product had not given trouble to the existing users. Thus, higher volumes mean a greater chance of building a higher customer base which results in improved brand equity.

1.1.4 Volumes improve the confidence of sales staff: There is a saying, "Nothing succeeds like success". The positive psychological effect of achieving targeted volumes on the sales staff is enormous. With improved volumes, the self-image and image among a team get a facelift.

1.1.5 Market share: If the volume increases at a rate higher than the improvement in market demand, it reflects improved market share. Improved market share gives positive pressure to know the causes which helped the improvement. This, in turn, helps the team to improve upon the momentum further.

1.1.6 Volumes infuse an electrical flux: The entire team oozes in confidence with positive energy engulfing the team, helping an improved atmosphere after achieving targeted volume.

1.2 Cash flow

If a decision has to be taken between a sales promotion process that is expected to bring cash flow immediately and the one which is likely to bring cash flows in the future, mostly the former is preferred over later. Cash inflow acts as the backbone of a company. Cash coming in from debts and other sources are liabilities, whereas cash inflow from sales is an asset. This asset is used to offset the liabilities. Timely cash flows are an invaluable asset to the company. Sales personnel who excel in bringing cash flows stand to be highly revered and treated as an invaluable asset.

1.3 Profitability

If the sales team has a better say in the company, if in a firm sales staff enjoy better and faster increments in pay, positions and the importance, it is because they bring in revenue, cash flow and have a hand on profitability by way of right price in the market.

For instance, when a company expands, increases its geographical presence, correspondingly the importance of sales staff increases as the dependence on the sustainability of the firm depends on sales department operations bringing in additional revenue and profitability.

Without adequate volumes, plant utility suffers and cost increases. The right price and volumes bring improvement in top-line (revenue) and bottom line (profits). Timely sustained cash inflow from sales supports the firm to run smoothly, pay debts on time and get supplies at the right quality and quantity at a lower cost. Thus, sales personnel devoted to volume growth, getting the right price and conscious of the collection, are an invaluable asset to the company.

1.4 Upholding systems

The market perceives a systematic, organized company, with well-behaved staff to provide quality product and services. The company with sales staff who talk with trumpet voice and announce their valuables, but have poor behaviour patterns and systems, will suffer in comparison with a competitor who has excellent systems and well-behaved staff. Advertisements and sales promotions work only up to initiating the customer to enquire and buy a product. A good product with operational systems in place, handled by quality staff, will gain the power of "word of mouth" spreading positive feedback from users in the market. This can have a greater impact than the advertisements and sales promotions.

The distribution channel which sometimes accounts for almost entire sales volumes of the company will prefer a quality product served by a systematized firm with a well-mannered quality staff. Realizing these truths sales personnel who act as the bridge between the company and the distribution channel or direct consumers, as the case may be, have to show full respect to upholding company systems, ethics and morality.

All other things being equal, if a distributor has to choose one out of two companies, he is likely to choose the firm with better systems and staff of superior quality. Remember, price adjustments and such other spot decisions can be copied by competitors, but the overall system and the superior staff quality cannot be copied easily. In the long run, this superiority apart from the excellence of the product will help a premium position for a company's brand.

For reasons seen above, sales staff needs to be consistent in having a focus on volumes, cash flow, benchmarked pricing and values upholding the company.

2. KDA to Serving Customer Needs

To achieve the objectives on hand for a firm, the market is the playing field. The market does not stand with welcoming hands to enable a firm to realize its objectives irrespective of what the firm does to the market. The market has needs. If the needs are satisfied, it is ready to give the returns.

The market is both oxygen and food for a company. After the marketing department had done the work of understanding the needs of the market, top management decides to produce the right product to serve the need. From this situation when it comes to converting this product or service to cash, the sales team takes on. Once on the field, the need for the sales team is to carefully review the acceptance and resistance levels for a product or service and then to make course corrections to move forward. If the reasons are within your control, serve it as only you can. On this service, let the volumes and collection become a by-product.

Imagine the market as a person to be taken care of for health betterment by a doctor. Consider yourself as the doctor. A contracted doctor has to do regular health check-ups on the patient for maintaining good health, to immune him from diseases or to cure diseases, if any. "Good health" of the market means, getting the sales and collection at the benchmarked levels. Keeping good health is to take steps to sustain performance. Immunization from diseases is to serve the market running the extra mile by which you make it difficult for competitors to break into your racks. Curing the disease is to take steps to correct the issues which choke the market from providing required sales and collection. Remember the key to all of these is serving the customer. The sales and collection should be a by-product of the service. As seen earlier, the client should feel that you are serving him and not selling to him. Even as you take care and show empathy to the customer, you stand to understand the needs to be satisfied, to achieve the objectives of the company.

The needs can be:

- Emotional
- Product-based
- Service-based
- Profit-based

2.1 Emotional needs

For emotional needs of the customer, what exists and got satisfied; what exists, but not yet got satisfied, requires to be understood. The emotional needs, when pruned down, may well end up as something to do with the image or standing of a dealer or end-user.

The salesperson needs to dig out the aspect on which the customer thinks his image depends on.

I shall narrate a small event to show how simple and yet deep can be the emotional needs of a customer.

A big cement trader in the business for over three decades carried with him a record for prompt payments without default. On one occasion, a field salesperson of a supplying firm by mistake made an error while depositing the payment given by this trader, resulting in the return of the instrument by the bank. It took enormous efforts of people at different levels to bring back the big trader on track. The emotional aspect of being "the perfect paymaster" meant so much to the trader; he was willing to even risk profitability temporarily and opting for alternate brands. Philip Kotler repeatedly substantiates the importance of emotion in sales-related transactions. This applies to both end consumer and distribution channels. For this reason, when handling customers an eagle eye is required to know their emotional needs and serve them.

2.2 Product-based requirements

This could be a feature-based or product type-specific, for which the supplier is expected to satisfy as promised.

2.3 Service requirements

What are the delivery requirements the customer wants and expects to be served properly are to be known. Any pending issues need to be followed up on priority. Strong understanding of the abilities of the logistics department of one's company, coordination with the logistics team can help sales staff to give the right commitments and coordinate for the supplies. On the other hand, if there is a delivery-related issue for the customer who is not satisfied by the company, and if the issue is out of the purview of the field staff, then the onus is on the sales staff to bring it to the knowledge of the management to resolve it at the earliest.

2.4 Profitability requirements

In the case of handling a distribution network, if there are bottlenecks with the profitability of the customer, it needs to be addressed. If the profitability of the dealer gets choked, then it is a matter of time before losing him. The issue can happen in any form. For example, a credit note that was due might have got missed out; mistakes can happen in invoicing, damages to be settled may be pending etc. All these can potentially affect the profit of the dealer.

Feedback on requirements of traders to management is important

Just as field force happens to be the ambassador of the company in the eyes of the market, the same field staff needs to act as the representative of the market needs to the management. Many times, out of fear of counter-attack from the management, field forces do not project the needs of the market. For this difficulty, the blame most probably lies with the culture of management not giving freedom of expression, bottom up. Management to know what is happening down the line needs to be connected inherently to the market through the field staff. In most of the companies, there is no separate team to work in the market to know the needs of the existing and probable clients. Except for a brief survey using an external agency, a thorough continuous understating of the market is missed out by many firms. In this context, the responsibility of taking the correctives for the market to the management rests with the sales staff.

3. KDA to Extracting Market Inputs

Albert Einstein said, "Small is the number of people who see with their eyes and think with their minds". This essentially means many of us do see things and events but miss out paying full attention to it to gain the required knowledge. Having an eye on what is happening in the market will help field staff take appropriate decisions.

For instance, for schemes and offers, unlike the automobile or FMCG industry, the details are not that open in building-material industry. It has to be dug out. Some sales people in cement and steel industry do believe that things on its own course will somehow come to one's ears and one need not be hell-bent on it taking initiatives. But if I see successful salespeople, they are eager and proactive to know the happenings and keep their eyes and ears open. They know the activities of the competitors and monthly demand dynamics. To monitor and evaluate the competition and to understand the market dynamics are actions to revolve as a continuous process with field staff.

How to disempower competition

Fundamental Knowledge of competition

Taking cement as an example, the given below inputs in the two tables are required for field staff for making a meaningful analysis of the market. Most of the details can be procured easily by quality staff. Consumption and profitability are the ones the field staffs have to dig out using network connections.

Brands, Distribution and Service:

Competitor	Source plant	Brands	Packing Type	Network strength	Retail Nos.	W.Sale Nos.	NT Party (No's)	Godown Numbers	Supply Mode	Avg. supply time	
										Direct	Godown
A											
B											
C											

Brands, Pricing, Volumes, Profitability (Discount):

Competitor	Brands	Retail Price of brands			Quantity			Segment		Profitability level
		I	II	III	I	II	III	Trade	Direct	
A										
B										
C										

Table 1&2: Basic data to have on market

A company's objective is to get a proper insight into the happenings in the market, and hence, it is helpful to structure the competitors to make analysis a little easier. Competitors can be broadly segregated into three categories for structured analysis. They are benchmarked competitors, standard competitors and disruptors.

Benchmarked competitors: These are the competitors in a market who have about the same size and retail price; have similarity in product features and quality, give nearly the same importance for sales volumes in the region.

Standard competitors: These are the competitors who are priced at a higher or slightly lower level. Adopt standard practices, systems, product quality, good service levels and pricing methods. They try to give value to their brands, try to improve market share through product or service differentiation rather than price. They may give equal or less importance to the market based on their profitability levels.

Disruptors: These are the players who are generally priced at the lowest bandwidth in the market. They frequently have an effect of pulling down the price level in the market. They may not give primary importance to the market and treat it as a dumping ground to improve capacity utilizations. Their presence, demand and pricing in their home market may have a bearing on their behaviour in other markets they serve. Some players even in their home markets will be at the lower end of the price band prevailing in the market.

SWOT Analysis

Market environment dynamics and how a company stands against this challenge can be understood in a simple yet powerful way by using a SWOT analysis. Market position analysis and customer profiling need to be seen in conjunction with SWOT analysis. This helps to design the right schemes to be implemented.

An example of a SWOT analysis of a market for cement

Strengths:	Weakness:
Commanding price position. Close access to market. Product type suited for market. Distribution network.	Long credit period. High labour costs. Complicated freights.
Opportunities:	Threats:
High infrastructure budgets. Increasing job opportunties. Increase in Urbanization.	Capacities to add up. Increase in freight costs. Increase in price gap with lowest brand.

Figure 4: SWOT Analysis of territory

Strengths: Strengths figured out for a company should always be with respect to the competitors and the customers in that market. Strengths must not be independent of these; as if independent, it will not bring results. For example, if the market has demand for 'slag' cement, and if the company has an excellent quality of 'ordinary portland' cement, the good quality factor may not get translated as strength. For a company keeping its price at the high end of the market can be strength or weakness depending on the acceptance level of the brand in that market. The strengths considered with reference to competitors or the needs of the customer alone are to be factored.

Weakness: Similarly, the weakness concerning competitors in that market and the customer needs including the service requirements in that market should be considered. If the market shares of low-end brands are very high in a market of high competition, a cement brand that stands alone with price kept at a high premium with a low market share can be a weakness.

Opportunities and Threats: These are to be seen from the perspective of risks possible from competitors' growth potential, profitability potential in that market and other such relevant factors in the market environment.

The political environment can be an opportunity or threat depending on the situation. A stable government with budget allocation for development is an opportunity, whereas an unstable government is a threat. The economic environment of inviting investments can be an opportunity while unionism and regular layoffs are threats. Socio-cultural clashes are threats, while peaceful culture is an opportunity. If the competition index is increasing it is a threat; if approvals for new capacity expansions are withheld it is an opportunity.

After knowing the market factors which are strengths, weakness, opportunities and threats, the next step is see in this background, what are your organisation's strengths and areas in need of improvement in that market (fig 5). The same needs to be done for competitors.

For example, for a competitor in a market which has high growth potential, average competition level, with good price positioning and profitability, but suffering from low distribution strength and poor logistics service, the radar graph would look as given below.

In this (fig. 5) case, the focus must be to increase volumes through increased distribution counters and to improve logistics. To correct these shortcomings relevant sales-promotional activities can be designed.

Problems for your brand, such as, erosion of the customer base may arise from any competitor; but the benchmarked competitor's actions may have an immediate effect on your brand. Hence, an eye on the benchmarked competitor's actions is even more important.

Strength and weakness graph

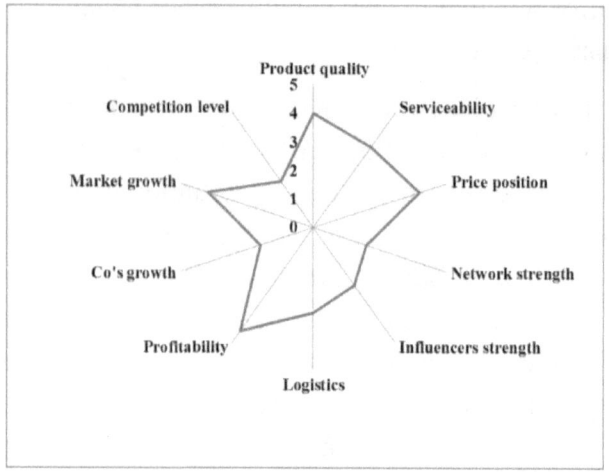

Figure 5: Example radar graph of strength and weakness, rated on a scale of 1 to 5, where 5 reflects highest

An effective way to understand competition is to study them from the perspective of customers. Normally, competition is read at a gross level, by way of volumes sold, market share, product type sold, segment focused and then left at that level. In many cases the competition is analysed only after facing some issues, such as losing the sale, reduced counter share, drop in customer base etc. Experienced staffs sometimes take competition for granted and feel there is a pattern with a competitor, and it will be handled when needed.

A competitor is to be reviewed on the following lines when looked at from the customer point of view. Customer point of view is suggested because if a competitor manages to see an opportunity, it will be easy for you to prevent your customer from getting poached, as the gap is seen from the customer's perspective. This gap or opportunity means the customer is possibly ready for the needs to be addressed and get converted.

For example, when Toyota decided to withdraw one of its model Qualis from India, it was a ready opportunity to competitors, such as Mahindra who had vehicles catering to the same segment of users who used Qualis.

We shall see some of the ways to study competitors from a customer point of view.

3.1 Product

The quality of the product serves certain utilities. Competitors' products in the market- particularly that of the benchmarked competitor- requires to be studied from this perspective. In case of variations, it can be used to either improve your company's brand or use the depreciation in quality standards of a competitor to improve your counter share, and market share.

For instance, in cement and steel industries a product output depends on the quality of raw materials. For a company, quality of raw materials depends on the quality of deposits in the mines associated with a factory. The deposits in mines may be inconsistent or deteriorating over time. In such a case, unless the manufacturer takes adequate measures, the changes in the raw material quality will have a bearing on the quality of the finished product. This effectively means, same brand when comes from different plants need not necessarily be of same quality.

In the cement industry, for instance, quality aspect can crop up in blended cement, as the blending material is outsourced from different suppliers, and the percentage of blending also plays a role in the quality characteristics of the finished product. If a brand is known to be higher priced and seen to deteriorate in standards, it is a welcome opportunity to capture a portion of their market share. The fluctuation in quality can be more frequent for a company which outsources clinker to manufacture cement. In case a brand of similar quality is higher priced, then it allows exploring if your brand deserves or has feasibility for a higher price positioning in that market.

Analysing competitors on quality, consistency, pricing and volumes as a combination gives scope for taking a lot of constructive decisions. You need to remember, if there is deterioration in the quality of the competitor, and if you bring it to the knowledge of some deserving counters, your relationship with the network stands to get strengthened as you are protecting him from possible embarrassment from his end consumer.

After having the ranking of competitors, as in Figure 5, the next step is to deep dive to figure out the areas to attack competition, with what I term as "relationship analysis". Since the majority of sales come from the distribution channel and influencers, relationship analysis becomes crucial; which has been taken up in the following sections.

3.2 Bonding level of competitors

After deciding which of the competitors to benchmark, how close a competitor company is to their customers is important. If the level of the closeness of a competitor is high, then it gives impetus to improve your standards with the clients. If the competitor develops gaps, it becomes an opportunity to entrench into the customer base of the competitor.

In case if the closeness is due to the nature of sales promotion schemes, for instance, it can be an opportunity to review the effectiveness and methods of your schemes. When many schemes are perused, the knowledge can help you to come out with innovative schemes. There can be occasions when the reason for closeness can be for reasons you cannot match at your level; in this case, the matter may be addressed at an appropriate higher level.

For all these improvements' devotion to gain knowledge in the market, and put that knowledge into action becomes the key.

3.3 Care level of competitors

What is the quality of care rendered by the competitor? Care can be based on many aspects. As seen earlier, product quality is one; delivery, systems, the reliability of the company and such aspects which have a bearing in your market can be taken up.

If care taken by a competitor is very exceptional in comparison to your firm, it will become very difficult to break into the competitor's network base. On the other hand, it spells danger for the erosion of the customer base for your company. This makes it imperative to initiate necessary improvements from your side. As seen earlier, good care rendered to a trader lifts his emotional bondage with your company.

Some important aspects of care rendered or failed by competitors to the network can arise from the following.

- Frequency of visits by company officials.
- Quality and friendliness of company's officials during communications.
- Quality time spent with customers by company officials.
- If the customer doesn't have to remind issues, once addressed.
- Feel-good relationship levels maintained by company officials.
- Quality and diplomacy of language used by company officials in written and oral communications.
- A company keeping up the promises made to customers.

3.4 Quality of service

What are the service levels demanded by the customers in that market? How well competitors address and satisfy these requirements? Against this, how good is the service level of your firm? Service can be categorised broadly in the following parameters.

- The ease of sales process.
- Invoicing standards.
- Supplying fresh stocks.
- Timely release of statements of accounts.
- Clarity of statements of accounts.
- Delivering at market-driven time slots: some markets prefer product availability in the morning before 10 am, as most of the building-material orders transpire at retail shops in the morning.
- Quantity of delivery: different types of customers need products of different quantity levels, by way of packing sizes or dispatch quantities.
- Consistency of products: in supply and quality.
- Size and utility of trucks.
- Accommodation of use of own trucks for traders.

3.5 Adjustability

Service levels demanded by the customers can vary between industries. Building materials, such as cement and steel, need a high level of adjustability from manufacturers to customers.

The following aspects, for example, are noteworthy.

- The dispatches involve high value per truck and the stocks need storage.
- The invoices may have several breakups, such as the cost of product, freight, taxes and discounts.
- In most cases, discounts are given post sales based on performance against targets.
- A portion of the discount is set for annual performance, which means it will be credited after the running year-end.

- Moreover, the selling price to end consumers can be different from the nominated invoice price. In many cases, the selling price may be less than the invoice price, demanding credit adjustments to be done by the supplier to the trader, after knowing the actual selling price, which can involve judgment errors.
- If the product is perishable, sometimes damages can get delivered necessitating returns.
- Dispatches can be at multiple sites needing the truck driver's cooperation and adjustability with the customer.

These and many more complications related to size, product, distribution and financial aspects make adjustability of a company a major deciding factor between firms competing in the market.

What sort of adjustability issues affects a territory, may be peculiar and specific to the territory. To know and adjust accordingly makes a company enjoy a strong position in that territory.

Factors affecting a firm in adjustability:

- *Conflict of interest:* To earn quick access to a new market, or when launching new product manufacturers sometimes tend to allocate sales and service contracts to the same entity. For instance, a dealer for a company may also be a clearing agent or (and) transporter for the same company in the same location he is based. In such cases when the company expands at a later date, if other dealers in the territory ask for any legitimate corrective actions from the clearing agent, the manufacturer cannot command the agent as the clearing agent is also a trader, who helped the brand to enter the market. If the company has to take course correction by way of doing away with the service contract of the agency, then to motivate the counter as a trader will become a huge challenge.

The company may have to choose between adaptability for long-term presence versus losing volume in the short term. But managements, in a competitive environment, reeling under low capacity utilization levels, will succumb to settling for the current sale. Professional firms must from the beginning try to avoid encouraging appointments and issuing contracts that suffer from a conflict of interest.

If two contracts suffering from a conflict of interest don't run parallel to the same entity, it keeps the path clear to make course corrections when required. When understanding competitors, to what level they have encouraged "conflict of interest" needs to be figured out. This will help convert the customers of the competitor suffering due to the non-adjustability factor.

- *Gap in system:* Competitors need to be analysed for gaps in the system adjustability issues – some of which are listed below:
  - Problems in invoicing.
  - Dispatch inconsistency.
  - Problems of multi-point delivery.
  - Delay in issuing credit notes.
  - Entry issues with credit notes.
  - Problem of damages not settled.
  - Issues of failed promises.
  - Correcting the difference between selling and invoice prices.
  - Issues of supply from neighboring states in border areas.
  - Technical support not rendered.
  - Order process timings, inconvenience and delays.
  - Payment acceptance timings.
  - Payment methods allowed and bottlenecks involved with it.
  - Credit-limit problems for deserving cases.

- Credit-period adjustments in case of any emergency.

3.6 Resolving issues

Across companies, irrespective of size, popularity and having the latest systems and tools to run the operations, problems or issues arise with customers. The problems may arise in many shapes and forms to a customer. Average firms might view the issue as a common affair and try to handle it without much haste. Professional firms approach any issue with utmost sincerity and swiftness. If the issue is legitimate, professional firms take corrective actions on priority. If there is a trend of any issue happening repeatedly, then the systems and its "checks and balances" are tweaked to arrest such issues cropping up in the future.

Field staff will do well to know to what level competitors resolve issues for their respective customers. Having an eagle eye on these can give an all-important opening for a company. Sometimes, issues can be so sensitive, making the ability to resolve issues be a major factor for companies. (This is dealt as a separate chapter due to its importance.)

Example: There was a case of a big cement wholesaler of 3000 MT per month for a brand having issues of pending credit notes with a company. There had been some errors from some officials, which created the issue. To resolve the issue meant, some officials will get exposed to management for their errors, due to which the issue was left unresolved. A direct competitor struck a deal, saying they will compensate partly for the loss suffered already and convinced such issues would not occur to the big trader, thereby capturing him on his emotions. The counter was converted and also managed to increase volumes to over 4000 MT per month. After the loss of the counter, the issue escalated to the management of the earlier company, with ultimately the official involved in the errors getting exposed.

3.7 Quality of field staff

A popular brand with poor quality staff is not as dangerous as a less popular but quality product, handled by excellent staff. This is my reading across regions in the cement industry. If a company is a benchmarked one and its volume has to be poached to increase market share, then the field staff has to be on the lookout for any staff changes that happen with that competitor or any issue arises with the existing staff of the competitor. In a counter where emotional aspect plays a huge role in sustaining the relationship and getting volumes, a sensitive issue mishandled by a field staff can create an opening for a direct competitor.

Competitor analysis radar graph

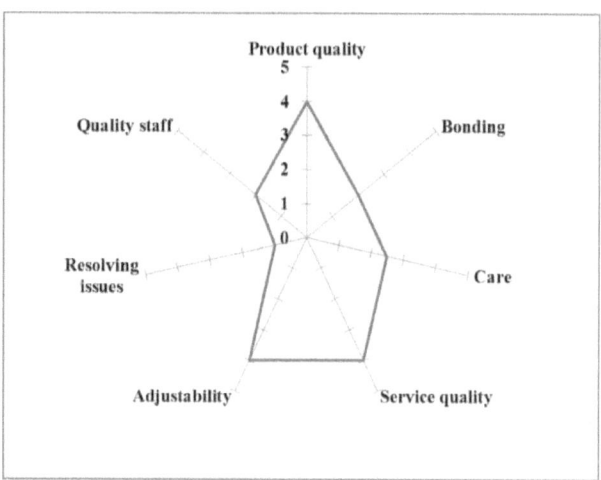

Figure 6: Example radar graph of a competitor based on relationship factors

For factors discussed in 3.1–3.7, an analysis of a sample competitor may look as in Fig 6, rated on a scale of 1–5, 5 being the highest rank.

The above hypothetical example is for a brand that has excellent product quality and service systems, but unfortunately handled by poor quality staff.

4. KDA to Utilizing Internal Strengths

Here internal strength refers to the power of tools available in a company to the employees to make full use of. All firms will have positive factors that can be used effectively in the market.

The strength can be derived from many factors, some of which are listed below:

- Product quality.
- Profitability to the distribution channel.
- Uninterrupted supplies.
- Integration between departments.
- Regulated systems.
- Brand equity.
- Result-oriented distribution network
- Deliveries made as promised.
- Quality staff of the required numbers.
- Advertisement support.
- Technical support for sales promotion.
- Accounts department support.
- Logistics efficiency.

4.1 Quality product

If the quality of the product vis-à-vis competitors is good, it has to be reached out to the customers. A quality product is such a wonderful asset, if the necessary impact is not created and goes un-utilized, it is one of the biggest tragedies a firm can incur.

We come across customers not being fully aware of a quality product served to them by a company. This is quite common when quality products come from public-sector undertakings. Surprisingly, even some private-sector firms do not make the full use of the advantages that its quality product can deliver.

If seen at a micro-level, the ability of a field staff to use the advantage of a quality product becomes very important as it can help get volumes at the right price. When an explanation is needed if field staff knows their product well, they can handle the situation confidently to overcome product quality-related bottlenecks.

In sales-promotional meetings, "get-togethers" at every given chance product-quality aspect must be squeezed into the discussion. Advertisement and sales promotion of a firm must succinctly bring out how excellent the product quality is. For instance, cement pricing has at least three cluster levels within the total price bandwidth that exists in the market. To hold a product at a higher price position and yet not lose volumes in the market, the customers must be aware of the good quality standards of the product.

That is to say, the product price must be viewed as "value-based" by the customer. Field staff should use good product quality maintained by an established brand fully and extract volumes in the market.

4.2 Profitability of distribution channel

Sales promotion tools, when designed for immediate returns, the objective is to help "push" sales. It can be for the short term

(3–12 months). Promotional schemes done to generate sales in the future beyond a year are to create "pull" for the brand.

When the objective of sales promotion tools is to "push sales", that is, for getting immediate results, it needs to be used diligently and swiftly. Sales-promotion discounts are such tools. If the company has designed it in line with the market with feedback from the sales department, it becomes an easy and a valuable tool to extract sales volumes. Distribution channel partners being business entities work for their profit. This makes an entrepreneur to regard the sales-promotion discount schemes as very important and hold it well imprinted in his mind.

The distribution channel broadly is of three types when it comes to handling their profitability.

- Entities that keep a thin margin and sell volumes to make a profit.
- Entities that have healthy margins without being aggressive on volumes to make a profit.
- The ones which strike a balance between the two by way of discounting for high volume customers to make a profit.

How and what to communicate to the particular counter depends more on the experience and judgment of the sales personnel.

Some manufacturing firms desirous of their products selling at designated prices may give part of discounts as a bonus and be less transparent in communicating the full discount structure upfront. By this, these firms try to make trade counters happy when the trade counters, at a later date observe that they have sold good volumes profitably.

Companies that feel their products get an additional sale by being marginally less in price try to be transparent in their discount structure, hoping the trade counters will promote sales more aggressively.

The majority of trading entities strike a balanced approach to make profits: discount price only when the volume is high, repayment is certain and the situation necessitates.

4.3 Integration between departments

A strategy that a company can hold, that competitors will find it difficult to copy, is to make the inter-department relationship butter smooth.

The coordination between departments must be well lubricated and act as pillar support to each other. After having a quality product which customer needs, making it known to the market, ensuring its availability, if a company has the culture of excellence instilled in the interactions between departments, the product will become almost invincible.

The sales force in the field must use it fully, if this parameter scores high in the company. For his part, the field professionals can make excellent friends with departments that matter for customer service. If the sales team manages this and serve their customers well, this by itself might well be a huge fort they construct to their territory from competitors, because a sales professional may in all probability find his competitor company suffering from severe politics and lack of coordination between departments creating a gap in service levels. The vindictive attitude within a company between people at the cost of customer service is quite a cakewalk for a competitor, as it is to his advantage.

4.4 Brand equity

Philip Kotler in the simplest possible terms depicts brand equity as the value-added to the existing product of a company.

Companies and its employees will do better to evaluate if their customers perceive their product as "value-added". It is not the value-added which the company wants to project, it is rather what is perceived, recognized and regarded by consumers that reflect the brand equity.

If I can say one element, if exist for a company with which they can play around with sales promotion schemes, squeeze maximum advantage when the demand is in an upswing, it is the acceptance level that the brand commands in a territory.

During company acquisitions, lot of importance is given to the brand or product acceptance in the market for the products of the target company to be acquired. Higher the level of brand acceptance, better are the valuations when bidding for the target firm. A phenomenon that helps predict future cash flows for a firm based on demand forecasting is the acceptance level a brand enjoys in a market.

Sales professionals must use this sword called brand acceptance to scythe through possible resistance in the distribution channel to achieve volumes. Sales professionals who are hungry for volumes will find "excellent brand acceptance" as an "Ace" factor for success.

Advantages of customer recall for a building material

- *Improve network base:* Good product inquiry levels can help increase the network base for a company. If a customer asks for a product, a retailer would prefer that he serves the demand.

When inquiry levels are good it becomes easy for a sales professional to approach a retail counter for taking dealership or sub-dealership as the case may be.

- *Cash discount schemes:* It makes cash discount schemes very attractive as the retailer will be confident of liquidating the stock quickly and thus buy the material on a cash basis to increase his profit.

If a retailer has the mind-set to sell to more customers, then he can use the discount schemes more effectively, if the acceptance level of a brand is very good.

For wholesale distributors, a brand with a good customer inquiry level is a huge advantage as they can recover their money faster from their retail outlets.

An experience of mine will be very handy to explain in this context. A wholesaler was doing huge volumes for a popular brand, in spite of complaining the margins were lower. A field official of another firm asked him curiously, as to why the trader does so much volume of a brand when the trader is not satisfied with the profit. The trader promptly replied as below, which gives valuable inputs.

- His retailers ask for this brand as end-use consumers demand it.
- Giving a brand which the retailer asks enabled him to collect his money faster.
- If for some reason a retailer is taking supply from other suppliers, he can use this opportunity to bring back the retailer into his fold.
- Using a popular brand he gets an entry into new outlets.
- He can use the retailer's counter to promote other brands of interest to the wholesaler.
- Being a top seller for a popular brand keeps the trader in the good books of his bankers

Thus, we can see popular brands are powerful tools for big wholesale distributors.

- *Labour turnover:* Labour turnover in the building-material industry is likely to be lower if a product has a good customer recall. In the building-material industry where face time with distribution channel or direct customer is likely to be high makes selling demanded products very satisfying to the selling staff.

  For instance, when a bigger and successful company acquires a struggling company with not well-established brands, employees of the acquired company had improved satisfaction levels in the Indian cement industry. A survey conducted for satisfaction levels of the employees revealed that a large portion of employees were unhappy with their jobs before the takeover by a bigger player. One major factor the survey brought out was the brand name of acquiring firm and the satisfaction of being associated with it had a deep imprinted effect on its employees. The new management could easily replace the old ones for the acquired employees. All these go to show making a brand get established with good recall contributes multiple benefits for a company.

  There are cases in the building-material industry where a company suffering from poor brand recall gives a good salary package apart from attractive designations yet failing to arrest the problem of increasing labour turnover across levels in the sales department.

  Just as success breeds success, satisfaction in job breeds improved productivity. Satisfaction in a job should not be mistaken for job security, which we see promulgates complacency and nonchalance in customer management in many public sectors. Here, job satisfaction means a satisfaction derived from the successful performance with a reputed product.

- *Extra impetus for sales promotion (SP) schemes*: High popularity level of a brand gives extra impetus to the SP schemes in comparison to what the same scheme can have for a less popular brand in the same location. With a powerful brand on hand sales-promotional schemes can be implemented more aggressively. Sometimes companies realise the need for an effective brand when they abysmally fail vis-a-vis competitors.

  Philip Kotler, while trying to explain the importance of consistent marketing efforts, elucidates he got a call once from a CEO asking Mr. Kotler to come and teach his employees some sales and marketing stuff as sales declined by 30%.

  The demanded product helps make sales promotion schemes attractive and evokes a welcoming response from retail outlets for the field person, making him have a feel-good factor selling a popular brand.

- *An edge during demand season:* In the building-material industry, there is seasonal demand fluctuation. Companies have to make hay when the sun shines, by achieving maximum when there is an upward curve in demand. A powerful brand has a better chance of utilising the upward swing in demand with a growth rate more than the market growth.

  For example, in the Indian cement industry, it is consistently observed every year, in the month of March, which is both demand season and last month of the financial year for most firms in India, powerful brands gain greater volumes and growth in comparison to brands suffering from poor recall value.

- *An edge if the price gap is narrow:* In the context of the price gap between the highest and lowest priced brands getting narrowed down than usual, the more popular brand known for quality and service will have an edge to eke out greater volumes by attracting the customers from lower-priced brands, as customers might well think if the price difference is narrow why not take a well-established and popular brand, as he is likely to feel more assured of quality, safety, and other parameters.

An automobile dealer explained this point with a classic example. The car models, one level higher to base variants, generally have more demand as a customer thinks by stretching a little, they get a better model, and willingly latch on to it.

In the Indian cement industry in B2C type direct party sales, a more popular brand with a marginal price difference stands to gain more volumes. In other words, if the price difference is narrow, the popular brand stands to gain in the B2C sales segment too, which is the period when popular brands should take maximum advantage of increasing their customer base. Builders who are into residential constructions prefer a popular brand to showcase that they used reliable materials and charge a premium in their bookings with the end consumer or to build confidence with the end consumer for charging higher prices for the property.

- *Helps revive a sick company:* Other things being normal if a company is sick due to financial reasons when restructuring is done to revive the firm the revival will be much quicker and faster, sometimes even remarkably quick, as I have seen from personal experience of being involved in one such case, if that firm has a well-accepted, established brand at its command.

The extra incentives on brand revival, if made attractive, and if the reviving firm can convince the market that the brand is well on its path to consistent supplies, can reap immediate results and positive cash flows to help its revival. The fund providers supporting the firm can become more lenient and cooperative with restructuring their finances if they are confident of revival with a well-accepted brand.

The Indian cement industry has seen multiple cases and situations in the events of mergers and acquisitions when purchasing firms paid handsome goodwill premiums for buying target firms with established brands and in many cases continued to use the brand names post-acquisition. M&A's that happened across the country saw this trend in the last ten years between the years 2009 and 2018.

There was a case of a sick firm closed due to insolvency. For its re-commissioning, the firm had to resort to strictly regulated restructuring with a pure cash sales model in the market, as the fund infused for revival was meagre. But to all parties' concerned - financial and operational creditors - the speed and alacrity with which market accepted the erstwhile established brand was a healthy heart-warming experience. The firm could even increase its price during the revival period and infuse better cash flows, which commanded more regulated supplies from operational creditors.

- *Helps to extract pressure sales:* In case of the need for immediate results, if the sales team has to adopt pressure sales tactics with tools of short term schemes, it is much easier for the sales team to achieve higher goals and targets, if it possesses an established brand.

4.5 Quality distribution network

Network mapping

At a micro-level, say at district, city, province, state as the case may be, the existing network has to be plotted. This helps to know what action to take for that territory, for developing the network. If you can do it to the competitors also, it can be of great advantage. But at least for your firm figuring this is mandatory.

Network status can be analysed from four perspectives:

- The total network of your firm accounts for a low market share of the territory with an average counter share of your firm being low.
- The total network of your firm accounts for a low market share of the territory with an average counter share of your firm being high.
- The total network of your firm accounts for a high market share of the territory with an average counter share of your firm being low.
- The total network of your firm accounts for a high market share of the territory with an average counter share of your firm being high.

Quadrant analysis of network scenario

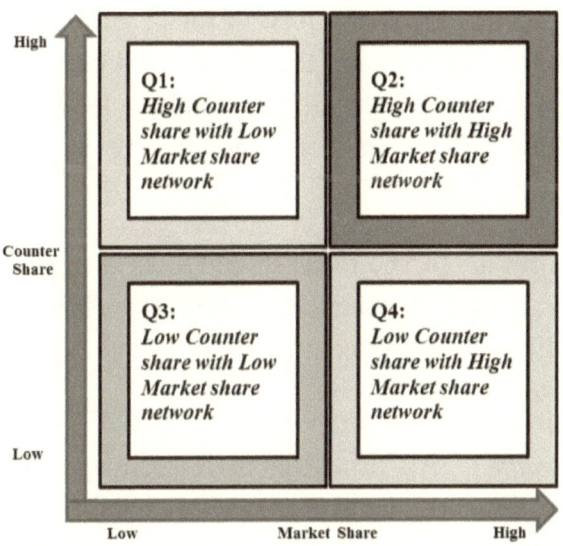

Figure 7: Quadrant analysis of network scenario

Based on which quadrant the network status of a company falls in a territory the sales promotion mix and marketing mix can be planned and executed.

The firm in Q1 needs to increase the number of high volume counters without sacrificing the existing network. This firm has been good at having a sizeable counter share in its network. What has been working for it to achieve a good counter share must be extended to more number of counters so that the total network accounts for a greater market share of the territory.

The firm in Q2 has a significant challenge to handle. It needs to protect counter share and the network numbers. It has to watch out for the increase in market demand and ensure the same is reflected in its network.

The firm in Q3 needs to have a high budget for sales and marketing mix to break the jinx. A lot of hard work needs to be done to change its standing. But the job will be very interesting if approached with the right attitude. From a lower base level, the growth achieved can be very encouraging to propel the firm forward.

For a firm in Q4, the focus should be in increasing the counter share, apart from protecting the network. Here innovation and deep understanding of the competitors is the key to exploit any opening that arises to increase the counter share.

Why this matters: All firms, for trade segment sales, rely on the distribution network. Unlike an FMCG company, where all the major outlets tend to have all of the demanded products, in the building-material industry, getting the best distribution network in a district or town is a challenge. A company in spite of efforts may not be blessed with the best of the network in all of its territories. In a competitive market, all competing firms cannot have the best of distribution network, because the number of capable outlets in a locality may be limited. If the available good ones are hooked to some firms loyally, then it becomes a problematic issue to push volumes for other firms.

The message: if your firm has developed a quality distribution network over a period, you as a field force need to take full advantage of it proactively. Failing to do this is a tragedy of sorts for your firm. The ability to use one's network proactively differentiates the successful sales personnel from others, even within a firm.

A firm that builds quality and loyal distribution network is like building a fort to defend a kingdom. If sales personnel are not alert to protect this fort, then poachers will run amuck to weed out counter shares to their advantage.

The distribution network is a collection of entities, which are business enterprises with a need for self-sustenance. If they have been loyal to a firm, it is an index of their happiness with some aspect of the firm they deal with. You, as a professional, need to understand this and make use of this advantage to get results, i.e. volumes, realizations and collections.

For example, in the Indian cement industry, in many locations - to name a few Mumbai, Bangalore, South Tamil Nadu and South Kerala - strong brands seem to hold capable and loyal network due to which competitors always feel the heat and find it hard to break apart the links.

If field professionals have a powerful distributor in a location, under normal circumstances, they need to take extra care and show alertness to serve and protect their counters, to immune their network from competitor's attack.

4.6 Short delivery time

In a given territory only a few firms with factories located nearby or local warehouse facilities can supply, say, a product such as cement, which is high-volume, low-value material, in short notice.

The construction industry is beset with projects without storage facility, requiring material in short notice. Retail outlets vary of losing a customer for supply reasons will prefer firms with a good supply record. Storing high volumes of products in retail shops are on a drastic decrease due to the increasing cost of material handling and freights.

In this context, the supply capabilities need to be beefed up, proactively planned, coordinated and communicated in clear terms to the customers. This can help take advantage of existing warehouse facilities.

In a single-tax system, such as GST in India, it is cost-effective for firms to supply directly from factories. But unfortunately, factories may be far away from the market. In such a case, planning, and logistics coordination and support are required to appropriately handle the supply requirements of customers to keep up the sales momentum.

4.7 Face time with customers

If a firm is endowed with adequate manpower to meet the clients in the market, then the fieldwork scheduled to have more customer face time will be a huge advantage. If a competitor has less manpower, then the number of calls possible can be less for that competitor. Quality and lengthy face time with clients is an invaluable asset for field personnel. It helps in many ways, such as the following:

- In gaining market knowledge.
- Improving relationships with customers.
- Address service issues at the earliest.
- Resolving issues meticulously.
- Protect counter share.
- Increase customer base.

When I was discussing with different seniors in the Indian cement industry on different issues affecting the industry, one issue which was common to many of them was the difficulty they face in motivating the field staff to make more visits to existing and new counters. To change this attitude, it will do good to appreciate the above-referred advantages of customer face time.

The Unique Advantage in Cement Industry

I see uniqueness in the relationship feasible with the distribution channel in the cement industry, which applies to a few other building materials too.

In the fast-moving consumer goods (FMCG) industry, the selling areas are demarcated to the field officers. Companies have a record of all the retail outlets. Religiously on specific days of the week, routes are scheduled during which the concerned field official has to visit all the retail outlets. When I was in FMCG handling retail, there were days when I made 40 retail visits in a day. There will be a lot of retail visits in the FMCG industry with less time at your disposal in each counter.

In pharmaceutical products industry (PP), representatives are required to meet almost all the existing medical practitioners in the territory, which gets recorded. In the PP industry, the need and time constraints of the medical practitioners will decide what length of time field officials can spend with the prescribers (medical professionals).

When we consider consumer durables (CD) industry, the structure is such, there will be very few big outlets as dealership points, particularly in small towns. In some rural towns, there may be just one outlet. This gives direct opportunity and a necessity to spend more time with the distribution counters, but the number of outlets to be visited is far less in comparison to the FMCG or PP industry. There are also no hassles in the CD industry such as large warehouses at multiple locations with heavy-duty logistics like in a cement industry.

The number of calls to be made during field visits in the cement industry falls in between the requirements in FMCG and CD industries. The time duration in a counter is more than the FMCG industry but less than the CD industry.

In cement industry, there is by default a need for "give-and-take" relationship between distribution counters and field officials. In FMCG and PP industry, the retail outlet or the medical professional, as the case may be, are more likely to have an upper hand when handling the respective company officials. There may not be frequent situations when they require return support from company officials for small issues. In the cement industry, for example, from the company's side, several soft factors are important for the trade distributors. Some of the factors can be listed as below:

- Timely supplies are important.
- Logistics complications involving labour, traffic issues, truck breakdown and seepage during rains.
- Post-sales credit note disbursements due to the distribution channel differ in quantum, frequency and transparency.

- Wholesale pricing and discounts transparency is a continuous tussle.
- Seasonal fluctuations of the market price, both ways - upwards and downwards - is a given thing.
- Handling perishable, yet non-returnable products can create sensitive issues during the monsoon season.

From the above-listed soft factors and such other factors, field officials of the cement industry are relatively treated with better mutual respect by the distribution channel. The relationship becomes such that both sides need each other's link frequently and one cannot predict when.

This makes regular field visits and matured handling of trade partners a very important factor in the cement industry. If field visits are not regular, trade channel feels left out, not being clear how to address issues when problems loom. If field officials are trained in handling trade partners in a diplomatic yet effective and understanding manner, it will be of enormous value to cement firms.

Field force, hence, should be motivated to make as many retail visits as possible during the fieldwork. Equally important is the quality time spent with the trade partners (Retail and wholesale distribution points - both existing and probable ones).

These efforts are something that has to come more from the attitude of the field official and once got and implemented will help field official in getting well noticed and appreciated in the market, helping him to achieve higher volumes and timely collections. In the last few years, the use of mobile-based applications to monitor field movements has increased among cement companies. Sales teams should welcome this to improve productivity.

4.8 Media Advertisement

Management guru, Peter Drucker comments, the best way to kill a brand is to advertise the brand which delivers a negative experience to customers.

For instance, if customers take the initiative to inquire about a brand after getting influenced by an advertisement, but find the product which is supposed to be available, not available, it leaves a negative experience. In such cases, the expense incurred for advertising in that territory becomes a colossal waste. In a competitive market with easy to switch over products, next time when the consumer comes across the advertisement from that firm, he will not pay heed to it, even if the product becomes available. Sales teams, for this reason, should ensure adequate availability to help build the brand, if the brand enjoys advertisement support in their region. Else they will create such a negative experience for the consumer that future advertisement will not give the needed returns.

Many firms in the building-material industry cannot and need not have extensive media advertisement support. If you consider the cement industry, the presence of the brand across regions and the size of the company play a huge role in selecting the media for advertisement support.

A brand present across the country can afford and find it valuable to advertise in media that covers across regions. Regional players with 10% or more of market share may find it valuable to reach to the customers through the media which is confined and appropriate to that region. A small regional player with a market share in low single digits, due to their plant capacity limitations, might try avoiding costly media campaigns, instead using only hoardings and displaying paintings in vantage points.

In such situations, the sales department needs to fully use the level of advertisement support that exists for the firm.

4.9 Technical Support

Technical support can play a significance role in the cement and steel industries. We have seen earlier retailers, and therefore, wholesale distributors prefer brands which customers enquire about.

From the point of building a relationship with the distribution channel and to show care for them, meeting their end consumers to explain the usage of the brand, its advantage, knowledge sharing of safety factors etc., is progressively required. This helps to make the end consumer happy, get a "feel-good" experience and inquire about the brand again.

When I discussed about this factor with many friends of mine in the cement industry sales operations, they had a common view, i.e., if the technical support team is not going to increase customer inquiry or repeat purchase, then the team is best described as off track.

Unlike electronics, automobile, plant and machinery products, the technical support in cement is not to repair or maintain a product after purchase. Cement is one of the materials used by the consumer along with other items. Hence, before it is used, explaining how best it can be used becomes important.

After a product is purchased, the initiative taken to meet the customer at the earliest to help the customer makes him realize that he has made the right choice and help him to use the same brand for the full construction process gives multiple benefits. House constructions come in a cluster, which means a brand used for full construction by a site has a high chance of influencing the other new houses coming up in the locality for the same brand, as the new upcoming house owner might feel more confident with a brand used before his eyes.

As the economy moves forward, with new construction techniques coming to the fray, having a strong, knowledgeable technical support team to reinforce the goodness of a product such as cement or steel will be extremely useful for companies. Civil engineering techniques are evolving and get easily shared between countries. More and more buildings and structures with innovative designs and special needs are on the rise across cities.

In this development scenario, technical support by way of convincing a big construction site of the appropriateness of the brand to serve the specific need becomes critical. This service rendered by a qualified technical person gives credibility for the detailing. If the civil structure requires a certain combination of materials, then giving the appropriate explanation to bring out the precise requirements for the customer can be a deciding factor to choose a brand. If a company has good technical team support, then the sales team has to work in conjunction with the technical professionals to process the leads to generate sales. A brand gets built if more customers buy it with confidence and feel good after the purchase.

Technical Team as Sales-Promotional Tool

We have seen influencers, such as civil engineers, architects, contractors and masons play a very important role in enabling the consumption of brands. The major advantage of using sales-promotional tools to these influencers is the focus it has on the right target audience, unlike media advertisement support which airs the brand far and wide expecting to initiate purchase decisions, brand awareness or brand recall. Focus on the target audience being one of the main advantages of the sales-promotional campaigns, it becomes fundamental that the target audience is chosen carefully and tracked for post-campaign purchases.

In the interactions I had with the sales experts in the Indian cement industry, all of us felt this discipline is found wanting in many locations. Sales promotion campaigns sometimes are done to appease the local dealer(s) than for the primary objective for which it was programmed. The technical team which is meticulous and systematized, targeting the right audience and later tracks the effectiveness of its campaign is a pillar to the sales department. While such focused campaigns are done, new leads come which can be used by the sales team. If the sales campaign had been done to the influencers attached to a dealer, then that dealer can be followed up for additional orders, which can help increase counter share. In the long run, this improves brand equity.

Added benefits of technical support

- Individual houses in rural areas are mostly constructed by way of the house owners buying the materials themselves. If the technical professionals of a cement firm build rapport with such customers, there is every chance that the customer will be loyal to the brand for the entire project and spread by word of mouth, of the value of the guidance he got and the savings obtained. This can help sell the brand at the right price as the customers purchase seeing the value and not price.
- When a new advanced product or a technically specific product is introduced by a firm, for a specific segment, the campaigning by technical experts becomes a must, to make the customer know the unique aspects of the new product. Invariably a special-purpose product is introduced at a higher price, which makes product difference mandatory to make customer accept a brand on its value. If a customer does not see

the added value, then he is likely to make a purchase decision based on price.

4.10 Sales Accounts Support

Attitude of sales accounts has a significant bearing on the market for the building-material brands. Buyers are institutions or business enterprises or government departments. This makes clarity, speed, efficiency, accuracy, in account statements important. For this, the attitude shown by accounts staff to customer calls has a direct impact on the relationship with the customers. With good accounts department's support, logistics efficiency will be better, as fleet providers will cooperate better in serving the customers. If a company has developed a good accounting system, able staff with the customer bent of mind; sales teams should use it fully to improve the relationship with customers to get results. If a competitor suffers in this aspect, a sales professional should try taking advantage of this weakness to acquire the customer base of the competitor. In the Indian cement industry, numerous companies have benefitted with excellent account teams and some have suffered loss in market share due to lack of responsiveness and responsible accounting services.

4.11 Logistics

One senior cement industry official said, from his past four decades of experience, he found more than 60% of the issues to be resolved post-sales had to do with logistics. Logistics accounts for about 15%–40% of the cost of a cement bag depending on the distance transported, scale commanded by the firm, and market price. With the onset of digital services, data collection and management improvements, and special software applications, logistics tracking has improved resulting in better efficiency.

The change is so phenomenal that companies that do not embrace improving logistics systems stand to lose in its market. Sales teams would do well to coordinate, cooperate and use guile skillfully with logistics instead of heated exchanges for the sake of customers. It is good to remember with efficient logistics in place order flows can improve. When an inquiry comes to a retailer, if he can guess properly the delivery time, the retailer can talk to his customers with confidence, honour his commitment and earn respect, which will help repeat orders. If the pattern is good, then the retailer himself will vouch and promote the brand which gives hassle-free dispatch service.

Logistics support can be in many ways

- Delivering at required time zone – morning, noon, evening or night as the case may be.
- Incorporation of mobile tracking mechanism for trucks.
- Trucks of required sizes.
- Multi-point deliveries.
- Properly covered trucks.
- Matured and flexible behaviour of drivers.
- Warehouse facility.
- Proper documentation.
- Loading trucks at permissible levels.
- Coordination with customers for swift movement to delivery sites.
- Segregation of good and damaged products in warehouses.
- Timely communications in case of unfortunate events such as breakdowns, traffic diversions, etc.

CONCLUSION

All sales professionals can develop the ability to succeed, as the requirements are not special born traits of a lucky few. The skills can be improved further with the right frame of mind. The core factors, namely Knowledge, Devotion and Application (KDA), are to be rendered in the four-pronged approach. The four-pronged approach, namely KDA to guideline objectives, serving customer needs, extracting market inputs and utilizing the internal strengths, helps a sales professional to excel in his functions from all directions. The values and habits embedded in the approach enables a professional to sustain great performance, both as a person, and in his function.

CHAPTER 7

ISSUES AS OPPORTUNITIES

OBJECTIVE:

- *To appreciate the importance from the organization's point of view to absorb issues arising from the market as opportunities. We have seen earlier when detailing the four-pronged approach that it is important to handle the problems that surface from the market. (Since the relationship with channel partners is crucial in building-material industry, I am addressing this separately in this chapter).*

TO VIEW ISSUES WITH A POSITIVE FRAME OF MIND

In the last decade or so due to the proliferation in the usage of the internet, sharing of knowledge, connectivity across the globe and technological advancement, there is a sea change in the way customers experience the products and services and the way they react to their experiences. With the onset of "24*7" customer support in service industries, the expectations from customers from firms to provide customer service has gained momentum across industries. This means apart from the need to have "24*7 cell" service availability, it should also be acting with speed, diplomacy, respect and resolving skills to make a company have a stronger acceptance level with the customers.

These changes in the society have an effect on factors determining customer-satisfaction levels and on the wide range of issues customers take up with the suppliers. Across industries and countries, customers demanding better services and appealing against the uncomfortable experience undergone are on the rise.

These make handling customer issues very important as mishandling can prove very costly. Managements with progressive approach help employees have an attitude to see the issues that crop up from the market as gates opening to help fine-tune them and enhance the business.

Two major factors influence customers to demand better service:

- Higher competition levels in the market, which ensures easy substitutes.
- Higher awareness levels of the customers.

CHANGING CULTURE

After financial, banking, e-commerce and mobile application services have created avenues to encourage customers to voice their feedback, customers across sectors tend to voice their feedback. My fair guess: out of the customers who suffer difficulty with products or services in the building-material industry, we can expect about one in three to give feedback on the negatives they experience. A decade back this might have been just one fifth or less.

THE NEGATIVE EXPERIENCE LINGERS LONGER

A medical practitioner with decades of experience said, he found his patients to express their negative experiences in their lives more expressively and aggressively than their positive experiences and seem to remember their negative experiences longer.

We can hereby infer that customers remember their difficulties with a product longer than good experiences. This makes it important to take steps to alleviate problems and make good experiences more exciting to help customers remember good times. It is now a requirement for firms to excel in addressing customer queries.

In spite of the changing needs of the time, some firms still see complaints and queries negatively. There is an absence of encouraging staff to see complaints as a chance to build a stronger relationship and to a possible business opportunity.

In emerging markets such as India, there is an increase in middle-class population, which means more disposable income warranting higher demand for products of superior value. When people graduate in financial status, their expectations for better service quality also increases. Customer service improvement has become vital to retain customers, to dissuade them from shifting to competitors. Customers legally are empowered more now with law amendments and new acts in force. For example, as per the amendment in the Insolvency and Bankruptcy code 2016 in India, a residential flat buyer if denied possession within the reasonable time frame, taking the stance as a financier, can file suit against the realtor. With increased awareness of their powers, customers are less prepared to accept sub-optimal products and services.

POSSIBLE REASONS FOR ENHANCED CUSTOMER POWER

- With improved and hastened travel facilities available for the middle class, people accommodate more work in their schedule due to which less allowance is available for delays and bottlenecks. These warrants need for hassle-free usage of products and services to customers.
- When it is easy to shift brands the customer is less likely to be patient.
- Governments' invite investments with attractive incentives in many industries which create increased competition levels. Increased competition brings with it several brands and players fighting to show their superiority. This enhanced quality of

service and products at competitive prices are the fallouts of competition.

It is important to see the possible reactions from the market after servicing a query to appreciate them and rein in a culture of excellence in service levels.

If a query remains unresolved

Let us take a case of a customer not being satisfied with a situation and having raised a query. Let us assume the company did not pay proper attention and failed to resolve. Here the customers can perceive the company being below par; they can get imprinted in their minds that their expectations were not met with. After such experiences they can:

- Stay with the company and raise the issues again to resolve.
- Stay with the company, but by voicing their concerns to other competitors in the market.
- Shift to other brands and voice their problems.
- Silently shift to other brands.
- Stay with the company grudgingly.

Query resolved

If the query is resolved with fairness, but only to average satisfaction levels, the possible fallouts are as follows:

- The customer can stay with the company and continue the business.
- The customer can still shift to a competitor to avoid such hassles in the future.

The second option means a company may think it has resolved the issue, but still lose a customer. Alternate choices abound in the market coupled with the impatience factor of customers, which makes a brand change a potential possibility.

Query resolved resoundingly

Here the customer is highly likely to stay with the brand. Senior executives in the cement industry feel over 90% of channel partners remain loyal to the firm if their legitimate issues are handled with fairness and consideration by the respective firms. There is a chance that the customer may be more connected to the firm than before the issue arose. If customers get to understand that the company has solved in such a resounding manner that the problem is unlikely to repeat, they are likely to be overwhelmingly satisfied and advocate the brand to others. Such customers may become loyal to the brand if they are helped to appreciate that the problem that arose in the first place was more of an aberration or humane in nature. This sort of customer can behave as a brand ambassador with his links in the market.

WHAT IS AN UPSTREAM ISSUE?

In the simplest possible terms, I can say an issue for a customer is the difficulty faced by a customer. This may be a perceived difficulty, a case of wrong understanding or legitimate difficulty. But it is important to approach it sincerely and act upon it.

WHY CUSTOMER QUERIES SHOULD BE TAKEN SERIOUSLY

In spite of the increase in customer queries, you will do well to remember only a part of the unsatisfied customers takes the initiative to raise the issue with the company. It naturally follows that when an issue arises, more customers might in effect be affected by the issue.

The possible reasons for not raising an issue can be as follows:

- It may be that a customer when raised a complaint in the past the issue was not resolved and might have formed a mind-set that issues hardly get resolved and will not voice his issues unless it is serious enough to make him stare at losses.

- If a company does not have proper contact details explicitly put, then it might be that most of the customers do not have a channel to express their issues. For instance, when I had problems with the power back up unit in my residence, I tried to contact the customer service officer, but there was no response. Then I had to search on the web to know alternate numbers to contact. All customers will not take the initiative to dig out alternate numbers unless the issue is alarming.

- If the process for registering a query is complicated, then customers may abstain from raising their needs, make their questions addressed or make their point of view known to the management.

- The culture of response from the concerned company may be hostile, making the customer to silently change brand at the slightest of hitches with the firm.

- Simply the customers who are business entities have very little time to take up matters with suppliers. These types of customers may have a culture of rejecting suppliers with a poor attitude for serving clients in the future. It may become a case of the gate closed permanently for a supplier.

THE FOLLOWING ARE POSSIBILITIES A COMPANY SHOULD NOT IGNORE

- There is a distinct possibility that customers who had negative experiences without complaint had swiftly changed the brand.

- If an issue is raised and goes unattended there is a greater chance of the customer changing the brand.

- If the issue had given real strain, the customer might never deal with the brand again. This closes the avenue for regaining the links with the customer.

- An unresolved issue means giving an existing customer on a silver plate to a competitor, who will accept it gleefully and use it to improve his standing and reduce the brand equity of the brand which lost the customer.

- For all firms, leakage exists by way of losing customers for various reasons. Some existing customers change brands for reasons beyond the control of the supplier, but if the queries raised are not addressed, this loss percentage will surge manifold bringing decline in sales. Company and brand grow when the volumes from new customers and existing customers exceed the volumes lost from some customers.

- Suppliers need to absorb some market information from queries raised to improve their products and services. Without feedback on issues, the real root cause of problems will remain dormant, allowing a competitor to exploit the weakness to his advantage. Unresolved issues if serious can bring huge losses from suits and claims.

- Excellence in handling customer queries can give an emotional boost to the customer and also help the concerned employee of the firm have the psychological strength to handle bottlenecks in the future. The knowledge helps in preventing the same issue erupting again. The employee's confidence can spiral up giving him greater poise and confidence as an individual. This effectiveness can save costs and provide time for more constructive work, for both the firm and the customer.

- Sometimes when the root cause becomes clear and identified, if the causes are within the control of the firm, the issue can be rectified permanently. If eyes and ears are open, a deep foundation can be laid to set good standards by the company which competitors may find very difficult to copy and hence can become strength for the company. Thus, in a way, it can be inferred that costs and efforts put in resolving customer issues can be an investment, bringing returns in the future.

- The first step that a firm can take in accepting queries is to make it easy for the customers to make one. With the onset of e-commerce proliferation in the economy, there is a culture of expressing positive opinions, negative opinions and needs by the customers.

One simple tool adopted by many companies is to put the toll-free number and email id in the packing of the product to make it known to customers that it is easy to reach the firm when the need arise.

To achieve excellence in the sales domain we shall look at the ways sales professionals can adopt when handling customer-related issues.

MAJOR PRACTICES TO OBSERVE IN HANDLING CUSTOMER QUERIES ARE AS FOLLOWS

1. Listening.
2. An eye for the solution.
3. Follow schedule religiously.
4. Update the customer.
5. Complete with exuberance.
6. Use the efforts.

1. Listening

Affected customers suffer in two ways: one is a difficulty with a product or service which may have a financial impact, second is psychological pain. Apart from these two difficulties, a customer makes efforts and allots time to make his difficulty heard by way of raising a query. Hence, it naturally follows that he will expect a decent hearing. Suppose the psychological difficulty the customer suffered from the product or service had been one of embarrassment or insult from the third party he will be under emotional stress which can trigger anger. When a person is angry, he might not be logical and considerate in his approach. If a field executive does not pay heed to the psychological pain of the affected party, then the chances of resolving the issue become slim.

Emotion is a double-edged sword as it plays an important role in making a dealer staying with a brand or severing ties with a brand. These can happen out of emotion. In the former, the emotion works positively, whereas in the later it is destructive. This is true for end consumers too. Such trying situations if handled with empathy and care giving due weight to the person concerned and then going to the logic involved in the issue might bring a turnaround in the relationship and forge a long-term association.

The discussion with an affected person should start with an apology for the situation the customer is in.

Habits which help listening:

- Start with an apology for the situation the customer is in.
- Listen actively.
- Dr. Steil, the founder of International Listening Association, gives an important observation. He says listening is a function of one's ability to listen and willingness to do so, that is: $L=A+W$, where L is Listening, A denotes Ability and W Willingness. Ability here does not mean some special skill set, it just means having auditory and vision organs - ear and eyes - put into function. Willingness is the will one has to listen to. Willingness to resolve the problem by understanding the issue at a micro-level is required.
- Maintain eye to eye contact with the affected person.
- Keep away from all distractions such as social media websites, peeping into mobile apps, emails, and messages.
- When a customer speaks do not start programming in your mind what you should talk next to the customer. If this instinct is not controlled, the mind programming what to talk next will not listen to what customer explains and miss listening to some crucial inputs. If the customer is to be understood properly, listening without distractions arising from your mind is crucial.

The earnestness will also convey to the customer that you are taking his issue seriously.

- Avoid interrupting the customer. In case if your communication is required, request the customer and then convey.
- When your turn comes please make open-ended questions, helping customers to speak out.
- Avoid defending blindly that your side is right and customer is wrong, even if the customer is wrong.
- Mind your posture as much as possible - whether standing or seated. Try to hold an upright posture which helps alertness of the mind.
- While leaving, better take permission from him and then leave.
- Remember, a customer is a company's property - not yours. This implies you cannot try applying your likes and dislikes on him.

Customer needs

To know what the customer expects is very crucial. Recently, I had paid the monthly dues to the mobile data service provider within the time limit. But the service provider kept sending messages that I had not paid and immediately at the end of the due date severed my connection. I emailed customer care with proof of payment. There was a response email mentioning I can expect a call back within 24 hours, but the attendance did not transpire. I sent two more emails but got the same results. I called and got to speak with customer service only after several attempts. The customer service representative was keener to say it was a system error from their side and did not appreciate the difficulties I had to go through. Here in this case taken as an example, what are the things I was looking for?

- I was looking for a quick and fair resolution.
- I wanted the service provider to take my issue earnestly.

- I wanted them to resolve and do it with ease.

The lesson is customers want fair resolution, done quickly with kindness and empathy.

The feedback I got from the direct parties, trade partners and influencers suggest the customers expect a response if via email within a day; if via telecom, availability of a responsible individual at least during working hours. In the building-material industry, the customers are more comfortable in explaining things in detail over the phone or better in person than writing detailed letters and dropping emails. This makes calling or attending the affected parties, either in person or over telecom, a vital step.

Accessibility of field executive

Sales professionals across levels must make themselves available, to be communicated easily. Many firms have toll-free numbers to take down the issue and refer it to the concerned executive to attend. The ideal should be the field personnel develop such a culture and personality that the trade channel partner who needs support contacts him first. If the field person has developed this affinity with the market, it is an index of his work ethics. A sales manager can afford to consider this as a positive aspect of his field force. I frequently find middle-level sales managers expecting the customers to call them directly for resolutions. But this will affect the entire system. Sales managers must be available with easy access, but the culture, ability, and attitude in the team must be such that a customer has confidence with his immediate contact, the field executive to address his need. Higher-ups may be apprised of the developments, but the field executive must take the lead for resolution.

Quick response

One senior trader, who is in the field for over three decades, told me that his retail network does not get satisfied if the responses are delayed, even if the issue gets resolved. The retail network keeps on harping that their complaint was not responded quickly and the delay had made the retailers' relationship with the end consumer difficult and embarrassing. Since the majority of the sales volume (sometimes even 100%) for building materials happens through the distribution channel, response to their need is as vital as a company official would give to an end consumer. There is a tendency for field personnel to respond to direct consuming parties more quickly, but taking the trade partners for granted as they are in frequent touch. The reason can also be due to the field executive having some preconceived opinion of the trade counter.

Early response with responsibility creates a good impression of consideration for the customer, which helps give the right momentum to carry forward future discussions in an amiable mood. All issues cannot be solved immediately, but the quick response is within the employee's control.

Sometimes, a customer might have an issue which a field executive might get to know from a third party, say, a clearing agent or transporter, etc. In such cases, if the executive takes the initiative to call the concerned customer to take note of his needs and resolve it, the habit sets a wonderful platform for customer loyalty. It is this sort of loyalty that competitors find very difficult to break, which all field executives can experience.

Communication of time limits

If resolving an issue is expected to take a certain amount of time, say a week or more, then communicating the same in clear terms justifiably and ably can remove anxiety and expectations in the mind of the customers. Without this, the customer will have to make frequent calls to know the developments which will add to the negativity of the already affected emotional quotient. In the financial service sector, for example, some developments clearly say a certain type of queries will be resolved within a certain number of days, such as the time required to process an application for opening an account, time limit guidelines for transferring amounts, etc. The message is, clarity in time limits required to act is important feedback to a customer.

Map words and body language

Verbal communication and body language should not reflect indifference to the customer. Many times the intention of the field executive will be good, but due to not applying modified body language, the right tone and right choice of words the customer will perceive the handling as impinging. The attitude of care at the time of listening is crucial. For instance, if a mobile data provider erred in disconnecting service to a person, and when attending the complaint if the service representative reflects the least concern about retaining the customer and talks with a touch of nonchalance, the affected individual stands to feel more offended.

2. An eye for solution

With open-ended questions and discussions, different elements of the problem(s) have to be dugout. Then by mapping the different elements logically, the cause and effect of the issue and possible solutions can be worked.

Segregation of soft factors in complaints

In the process of unravelling the truth behind problems, it is better to know some behavioural aspects of customers when they raise complaints.

- *Leader styled*: Some customers who are senior in age and experience, make complaints with clarity and also have an ear for the words of the supplier. This matured behaviour is also associated with respect rendered for the human side of the executives of the supplier.

- *Subordinate styled*: Some customers who are not well-informed and a bit passive in nature are meekly styled while complaining. The reasons can be many.
- *Enemy styled*: Customers in this style are very aggressive and can be abusive too. The sensitivity factor will play a very powerful role when handling this type of customer. The customer may be confident and bold, may not be ready to give vent for humanitarian considerations. Might take a lot of cooling time before willing to listen to suppliers.
- *Balanced and philosophical*: This rare sort of customer may explain clearly and leave the responsibility to the supplier. These customers may be experienced and knowledgeable and confident in nature.

Irrespective of the type of customer, the supplier should not deviate from displaying professionalism in resolving the problem.

In this context my suggestions are as follows:

- From the past see how similar issues were resolved to get a cue.
- If the alternates suggested by the customer are ethically right and are in line with the practice in vogue, if within your decision limits, see if it can be accepted immediately.
- Earlier the resolution, greater are the chances of the customer getting satisfied with the handling process.
- If the solution is not clear, discuss with higher-ups.
- If the issue is complicated, handle as a team from your company rather than as an individual. In the case of a team if the issue is sensitive, you get the opportunity to have one senior to act as a mediator.
- See if the entire issue is based on some communication gap - as in that case, the same can be explained.
- When deciding how to solve the issue, look for the possibility of involving the customer.

- The issue has to be checked from different platforms:
  - Platform 1: If the issue is human related - based on human error, communication gap, an individual's expectations, etc.
  - Platform 2: If it was due to the process adopted - logistics process, sales process, discounting process, etc.
  - Platform 3: If system errors have caused it - like IT-related billing issue, wrong pricing, quantity mismatch, etc.
  - Platform 4: If the environment created the issue - like competition factors, existing profitability levels, type of product, services, etc.

The solutions may range from a simple decision, such as a need to reschedule a supply, to complicated course correction requirements, such as replacement, reimbursement, credit back and special approvals. The solutions which are within ones' limit are to be taken up and solved immediately. If the situation needs recommendations and approvals, then those course corrections to be set in motion at the earliest and the customer to be briefed and updated.

The negative power of assumptions

Making conclusions based on one's assumptions can be the root cause of issues. History abounds with kingdoms and nations ending up with war against each other after the actual issue started due to wrong assumptions constructed by one party or the other.

When one makes guesses at another's thoughts, one should realize that it is only a possibility that such thoughts might have been nurtured by the other person. This naturally means, there is a probability that such thoughts may not have occurred in the first place. But we unconsciously conclude what we assumed was right and start acting based on it. Then counter-reaction comes forth and then the chain of actions and reactions emerge. The lesson is that the entire issue might have started due to the wrong calculation.

This implies in a customer dispute, patience is required to unravel the cause, to know if wrong assumptions have played a role. There is an old proverb in India meaning "patience is bigger than ocean". The effective meaning is ocean silently accepts rivers and does not overflow. That is, a patient person can absorb pressure and maintain his originality.

After taking the inputs as above, they have to be mapped for links and causes to find a solution.

3. Follow schedules religiously

The following practices can be helpful when exercising solutions:

- While implementing the solution, a schedule is of the essence.
- Keeping up the schedule will give additional confidence to the customer.
- Extra care needed to avoid getting into an additional problem(s) during implementation.
- Always strive to keep up the promises.

4. Update the customer

- Communicating the progress to the customer is an effective way of showing care to the customer.
- This helps remove a lot of anxiety for the customer.
- This also helps keep the business afloat with the customer for volumes, collections and sales-promotional activities with his full cooperation, even as the solution to an existing issue is running parallel.
- This can help keep the competitors at bay from poaching your customer.

5. Complete with exuberance

When completing the solutions keep the customer in excellent relations so that he remembers the efforts.

6. Use the efforts in future profitably

Lastly, after successful completion, to make the customer understand subtly, the effort taken to resolve the issue is important. This helps make the customer realize and appreciate the efforts and have healthy business dealing in the future and spread a good name for the brand, company and the executives involved.

CONCLUSION

Handling issues that emerge from markets needs to be seen as an opportunity to refine ourselves and the standards of our services. At the corporate level, by taking up the issues as feedback it helps firms to refine and fine-tune the products, systems and services rendered and come out even with a renewed robust structure. An issue handled with utmost care and aplomb reflects the genuineness of the staff and the firm to construct a long-term relationship with the customers.

CHAPTER 8

PRICING PERSPECTIVES

OBJECTIVE:

- *To derive the importance of pricing and its methods.*
- *To peek into the effect of customers' perception of the brand from a value base.*
- *To take up the discounts and its related schemes to see its benefits and effect on retail prices.*

BASIC NEEDS TO FOCUS ON PRICING

Why does a company take so much care and analysis in setting up the factory, make investments in the best of machinery, decide on the process that is best to bring a quality product after deciding what product the customer needs, build robust distribution systems, pour money on brand campaigns, sweat it out to build relationships with the distribution channel and influencers? The unwritten objective is to see how best the company can reduce its products' dependence on price when it is purchased by the customer.

No market can be termed as perfect competition. Here perfect competition is referred to, in the sense of many products, available in the market without any sort of differentiation whatsoever between them with supply far exceeding demand.

In the building-material industry, particularly for cement and steel, price positioning has a huge bearing on the profitability potential of a brand. There are big size players who got their price positioning wrong for brands and could never recover for those brands. Recovery to better price positioning can be overwhelmingly difficult and costly by way of the need to introduce an additional brand or having to change the brand name.

COMPANIES MAKE PRICING IN TWO WAYS

The first method is to know the costs involved and keep a margin to arrive at the selling price. This method is termed as mark-up pricing. The other method is to go as per the prices in the market, which is termed as going-rate pricing.

Commodities trade at the going-rate method, but we will do well to remind ourselves that all products sold using the going rate method should not be termed as commodities. Most of the building materials, for example, cement, price products by the going-rate method. For adopting this method, certain level of market survey, background work and continuous monitoring has significance. Without the backing of these, if the going-rate is to be used, then the company may end up pricing lower than needed. This is because channel partners are likely to play down the price levels. If the price arrived at is lower than what the product is capable of commanding in the market, the difference is a direct loss to the company.

LESSON FROM THE AIRLINE INDUSTRY

For air ticket, business-segment travellers who travel based on need, emergency and appointment commitments do not pay too much attention to the rates. In case if it is a personal journey for leisure, the planning is done in advance and booked at the lowest possible rates. The facility in the airlines is the same for both types of travellers.

The lesson: when a buyer is willing to pay a price for a product or service, it should not be discounted. In other words, discounting a price should be done only where it is required, and at any given opportunity, better price should be squeezed out.

In the cement industry, for instance, there are broadly two segments. The pricing is different for direct consumers, as one segment, and retail buyers who form the other segment. Further, within the two segments, pricing differs between brands, which is the respective price positioning achieved by the brands. Companies should position their products with much deeper consideration than just segregating as direct and trade consumers, and then on that standpoint applying the going-rate.

If without adequate consideration, prices are adjusted, then the price itself becomes a sales promotion.

Good companies that want to improve brand equity and enjoy right margins adjust prices only to the right extent. With this discipline, they do not end up converting price positions into price promotions.

PRICE AND BRAND POSITION

For fixing the price, a simple and effective method can be adopted. This requires market transparency by way of the company extracting the right inputs from the market.

Attractive category (AC): If the quality of product, service standards and sales-promotional support are of high standards but is priced lower than other brands of relatively same levels in terms of quality and standards, customers may take it as an opportunity and buy, but the company will lose margins. Also, the brand will get registered in the mind of the consumers as lower than the premium-priced brands. In the long term, this will transpire into a huge opportunity loss. The pricing might look predatory in nature and may prevent the market prices to move up. If we consider the lesson from the airline industry when a brand can get a better price from consumers, the additional price should not be sacrificed.

Low-value category (LC): For various reasons, if a company has to compromise on quality, features and or some of the service parameters, then it has to make compromises and sell at relatively lower price levels to price leaders. Most of the brands if it gets into this groove stand to get destined to remain in this position throughout the product life cycle.

These brands suffer the most if its price gap with market leaders gets narrowed down. Another factor that suffocates brands in this position is when these brands have to cater to direct party orders. Direct to consumer orders are already priced considerably lower than retail price levels for all brands. Sometimes during the off-season, the price difference can be as high as 30% less than the retail price. In such cases, the price gap between popular brands and low-value categories will be less, due to which customers might prefer value category brands at a slightly higher rate. These brands, in the long run, get confined to be at the mercy of wholesale dealers for volumes or to the bulk buyers who are price-conscious.

Mapping price position

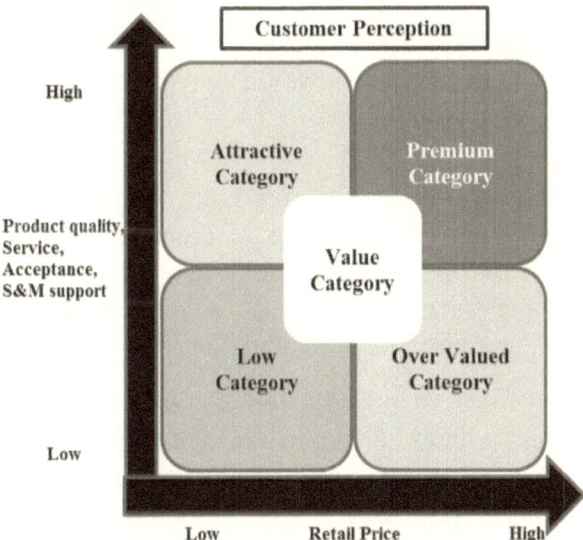

Figure 8: Mapping price position of brands from customer's point of view

Over-value category (OC): If a brand does not do enough course correction in quality, product needs or service requirements but keeps it premium priced, the customers are likely to perceive it as over-valued. These types of brands stand to lose volumes and brand equity quickly. If enough survey is not done, or if the sales team or marketing team does not dig out the reason for poor acceptance of the product, its decline will be just around the corner. Such brands will be easy prey for competitors, and such situation can also affect the morale of the employees. If sales professionals stand to lose sales to competitors due to inherent faults in the product or by way of wrong product which does not fit the market needs, they can find the job a huge psychological burden.

Value category (VaC): These brands float along with the market demand dynamics. These have a mix of trade and direct party orders; though in trade, there will be more dependence on wholesale merchants to push volumes. Sometimes if popular brands have to cater to distance markets, they adopt this price positioning for those markets. If the market-price levels crash or if the price gap between this position and premium level narrows down, volumes take a hit.

Premium category (PC): Well-managed companies that think of long term and invest in all aspects of brand health need to aspire this price position. These companies take care of excellence in quality, service, sales promotions, advertisement support and customer pull, to enjoy this price position.

These brands have less dependence on wholesale merchants, and sometimes, wholesale merchants will be dependent on these brands to satisfy some of his retail outlets, as customer pull will make retailers demand popular brands from wholesale merchants. Faster liquidation of a product will make retailers pay for their purchases earlier to a wholesale merchant. As cash flow is always an important factor, wholesale merchants will be forced to deal with popular brands.

Repercussions of the price positions

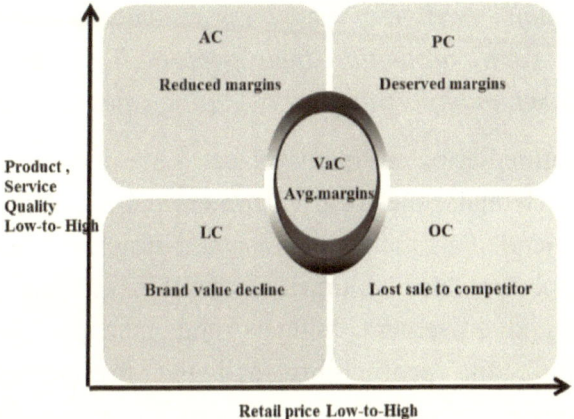

Figure 9: Effect of price position for a firm

Investing and making brands sit in this position can bring overwhelming returns for a firm. When authorized retail outlets of the company increases, then discount outgo as cost per unit for the company will drastically come down, because more counters mean average sales per counter will come down. For instance, in the cement industry, higher the volume sold by a distribution channel partner, bigger will be the discount to be given by the company. Due to this factor, if a popular brand improves its retail stockiest base, its average discount given per bag will come down which will add to the profitability of the company.

Employee morale will be better when they sell a popular brand and achieve targeted volumes. When market price crashes, these premium brands are the most insulated to survive the crash and recover fast.

During the demand season when the price gap with low-end brands narrows down, the increase in sales of premium brands can be better than the market growth rate, for that period.

117

DISCOUNT SCHEMES TO INTERMEDIARIES

When a major portion of a business depends on intermediaries, entertaining them, protecting their profitability, and generating push sales form an important part of getting sales volumes.

The intermediaries in many places have establishments for decades, which make the local customers believe them and what they recommend. This makes the discount structure a potent and a powerful tool for sales volumes. Even if a company has deep pockets for advertisement budgets and manages to establish customer pull, the profitability and the togetherness of the intermediaries are important to gain sales volume in the territory. For volume sector like cement, a brand with excellent customer pull can reduce its discount per unit of product and make the intermediary earn more by selling more volumes. But, the role of distribution channel and its profitability plays a major role in its success, in a territory.

Staggered discounts

In the building-material industry, for some products, this is one of the most popular schemes. Post sale, dealers wait for months or a year to get a part of their total discount. A major portion of the total discount earmarked gets bifurcated into monthly, quarterly, half-yearly and annual periods. The discounts are mostly based on targeted quantity slabs.

The expected idea: for products having high fixed costs, with plant demanding daily operations of sufficient capacity utilization for cost efficiency, consistent sales movement becomes important. When discounts are based on targets for different slab periods, there is a better chance of pushing orders consistently through the distribution channel. Moreover, when the amount accumulates, the discount figure to dealers can be a substantial value, making it look attractive when credited.

When a dealer gets money at a later date, there can be a tendency to sell a brand at nominated prices. If discounts are released immediately the retail counter may tend to cut the price, reduce his margin and sell. This can have two repercussions. One, brand value will come down. The other, the dealer will feel later, that he has not earned enough, and his margins are poor. Companies tend to perceive, if some parts of the discounts are released in a staggered manner, it is a win-win situation, helping volumes and retail price. This may help the company to hold the dealer, from getting poached by competitors. If the dealer's volume is high and the amount due to him is sufficiently large, this is one of the ways companies tend to believe they can bond well together.

There can a few more benefits, if seen from the company's perspective, with this approach.

- In case of default in payment by the trade counter, the risk gets mitigated to the level of discounts due from the company to the dealer.
- The amount held back, as a whole for the entire trader network, will be reasonably high, as a source of money for current business operations for the manufacturer.
- Some companies may not reveal fully what amount is held back only to release it at crucial situations making it look doubly attractive. This method can have the benefit of the retail price at nominated levels for such brands.

At the end of the day it boils down to what is best for a particular network to enable it provide in return the expected sales volumes, collections and profitability.

For small retailers with multiple brands, this practice by manufacturers can be a pain as cash inflows, by way of credit notes of their margins, are very critical for them. Companies can segregate the trade channel between small retailers, medium-sized dealers and big-size wholesale counters to modify the discount schemes accordingly so that the credits passed on to small retailers will make them comfortable.

Cash discounts

Cash discount means manufacturers getting payment for the supply within hours or a few days from the date of invoice for which a certain incentive is passed on. Some companies pay 25-45% of the total discount earmarked for a dealer as cash discount if payment is obtained within hours say up to 48 hours (2 days).

This motivates trade segment to give cash immediately and buy material to improve their profit. Both the retail dealers and cash rich wholesale dealers find this very attractive. From the company's point of view, getting the payment immediately improves cash flow and collection risk also gets mitigated.

There is also a psychological factor that comes into play:

- If dealers purchase paying immediately they have incurred the sales cost and will push the brand fast to recover the money at the earliest from the market.
- If a dealer has two brands one purchased availing cash discount and the other on full credit terms, when a customer walks in, the retailer will tend to push the brand for which he had already incurred cost. Hence, trade sales done in cash discount can psychologically make dealers to push a brand with initiative. Moreover, the retailer will, in turn, give only to reliable customers, which implies good, reliable parties would use the brand, which helps brand value.

Entertainment and gifts schemes

Many firms find this very valuable – to give benefits in kind instead of money to the channel partners. Dealers given their ways of getting locked in the maze of daily business routines, find it useful if companies arrange tours to excellent leisure spots, which left to themselves they seldom manage to arrange. When a partial amount is given as kind or entertainment, this amount loses its scope of getting reduced from the retail price and sold. This can result in better pricing at the retail level coupled with the chance of building togetherness with the dealers. Certain memories stand for life and companies like to capitalize on creating a wonderful time during leisure trips with channel partners.

Incentives

For influencers such as mason and builders schemes for repeat purchases by way of coupons or digital proof mechanisms are rendered. Influencers act as the bridge between retail counters and a major portion of end consumers. With individual house construction becoming rare in urban limits' role of high volume influencers have increased manifold. In semi-urban areas, too individual house constructions are done by giving full contract to builders. Even in case, the house owner undertakes to purchase materials himself, he does it after taking referrals, making influencers' role important.

Apart from the above, incentive schemes can be done in a variety of ways, according to the nature of the market and preferences of the intermediaries.

CONCLUSION

Pricing decision needs to be done after careful analysis of where to position the product in the market. Understanding the price position from customer's point of view is crucial, as it has a bearing on profitability for the firm and retaining (or losing) customers. If pricing is done dynamically, with sales volume alone as focus it peters down to "Price promotion". On the other hand, if the discount and other schemes rendered are given in regulated, monitored and controlled manner, it can go a long way in achieving nominated retail prices for a brand and also make the dealer fraternity and influencers happy.

PART III

LEADERSHIP: TRANSCEND TO GREATNESS

CHAPTER 9

LEADING FOR RESULTS

OBJECTIVE:

- *To deep dive into the four top qualities, which I strongly believe has become imperative for leaders in the sales function.*
- *To detail as to how the four qualities can be entwined with the four-pronged approach to bring out excellence in a leadership role, which enables one to transcend from good to greatness.*

BACKGROUND

After the effective performance in the field displaying many good habits and characteristics that bring results, people get elevations to higher levels. On becoming a leader, these habits are to be of great advantage but not enough. A leader in the sales function has to perceive him, as being part of the field force and guiding it. Taking the example of the cement industry, successful leaders have remained part of the field force and led the team as a guide. For the same reason people who, upon getting elevation who distanced themselves from the field staff, having an imaginary barrier and practised the idea of leading mainly by remote, suffered in the long run.

The extra element required, which is the key to be successful as a leader in the building-material industry as I see it, is to remain part of the team and take charge of the situation as a guide. This is true across levels. To remain close and be thorough of the needs of the team gives enormous strength to you and your team. We saw earlier the four-pronged approach that is required to excel as sales professionals. In this chapter, I endeavour to bring to you the qualities a leader can have as guiding forces to be effective in its implementation. The four-pronged approach forms the core and fundamental for success in sales professionals across levels, with the difference coming only in the way it is taken at each of the higher levels as you progress in the ladder.

FOUR IMPORTANT QUALITIES OF A LEADER

I believe there are four qualities a sales leader should imbibe in him. In each of the four, he has to apply the four-pronged approach for excellence. The qualities I believe a leader should rest upon are as follows:

- Faith
- Freedom
- Hard work
- Embracing people

Let us see how the four-pronged approach needs to be applied on the platform laid with the combination of the above four core qualities.

FAITH

Faith displayed on guideline objectives

- Conviction on the objectives of the firm towards
  - Volume.
  - Price.
  - Collections.
  - Rules, Regulations, Systems, Procedures, and Morals.

Qualities entwined approach

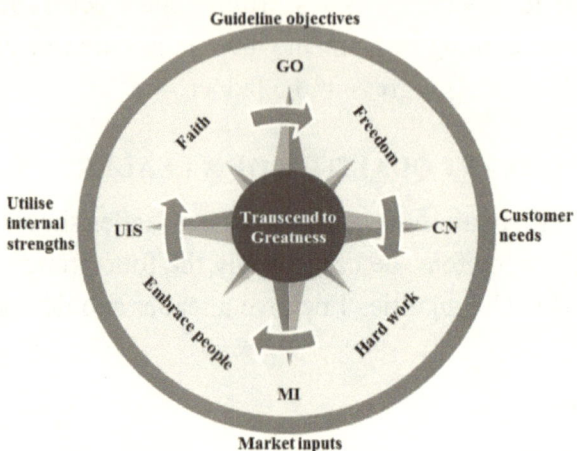

Figure 10: Qualities and approach entwined for greatness

Conviction on the objectives

A leader must realize why a particular level of volume is targeted. Just considering a given sales target quota will not work. Why that target is useful for the firm has to be realized.

Example: Suppose a company acquires another firm in the cement industry. The capacity of the firm formed by the merger of the two entities will be higher than what was before the acquisition. Suppose the target company was running at less than 50% capacity, while the acquiring company had bid and got with the aim to increase the capacity utilization to 75%, then the new target after acquisition has to be higher than the two independent companies achieved before the acquisition. This is because if the expected capacity utilization of 75% is not achieved over a period, the acquisition can end up as a failure. A leader needs to manfully realize the new target to increase the market share in the market. If instead, he is to come out with excuses for why the extra volumes cannot be achieved, then he will not be helping the management's decision of acquisition. The results might get delayed or may fall short of the target, but it should not be due to slackness in efforts.

A leader has to be convinced of the targets to help himself and his team to go all out towards achieving the target figures of volumes, price positioning, and collections. All three are embedded with each other. Trying one or two of these three will not help the firm in the long run.

Embedding faith in network

After following the systems, business sense applied in selecting networks and influencers, one has to back them to perform. Faith on extracting the best from your distribution network, loyal direct customers and influencers are very important. Sales promotions, incentives and strengthening relationships are all in a way to encourage them to perform better. When we encourage someone, faith must follow it to have its full effect.

Indian cricket legend Sachin Tendulkar once said he focused more on how to put the strengths to better use instead of infusing anxiety to the team by harping about the weakness in the team. This conveys a greater focus on the strengths helps bring good results. A leader has to figure out the strength of his network and focus on using it to the hilt. The sales promotion schemes at its planning stage need to take the strengths of the network as a solid consideration.

The strengths and weakness of every authorized dealer have to be bulleted, graphed and kept for constructive use.

An example of figuring out the network profile is given below.

An existing authorized dealer who has contributed to an increase in his retail counter sales, additional sale through influencers and from new retail counters can be graphed as below for four successive years.

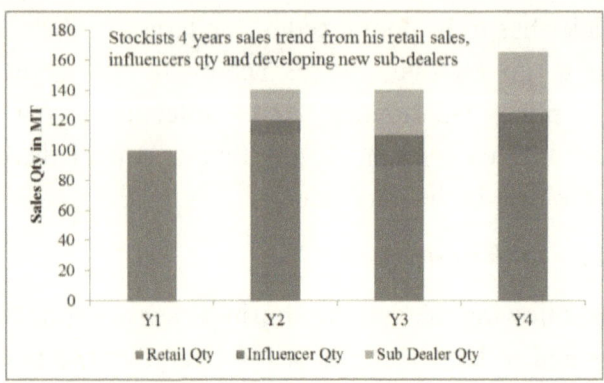

Figure 11: Studying a dealer's performance from the components of his sales quantities

There can be a tendency for sales professional to think he knows all aspects of the counters handled and charting as given above is not required. But in crucial moments, if you want to pull the strings on the strengths of dealers to extract performance, having their details in black and white as above will work wonders. What type of customers constitutes for the sales volume of a dealer is important information required to protect or increase counter share. Giving a sales promotion support accordingly based on the customer type(s) will give better returns for the sales promotion expenditure.

Apart from statistical data to know the strengths of a dealer, if you can know the soft strengths of major sales counters, as a leader it can be immensely useful. For instance, the way of connecting with his end customers might be the key strength for a counter; for another, it might be the payment or credit system they follow with the end customers. For another, it can be the service levels with the end customers and so on. If you are thorough of the strengths of the dealer and bring it out ably to him it can win a lot of admiration and appreciation unsaid with the counter.

Faith in discovering market opportunities

The leader has to encourage his team to get the much required market inputs. From the inputs how to connect the dots to derive meaningful observations can come only when the leader acts as a guide first and encourages his team members to joyfully come out with ideas.

Togetherness built on faith helps get market inputs: Just as a competitor is eager to poach your market share, you must be equal or better at the task. As much information as possible of competition and market developments are required to make the necessary adjustments and be proactive to protect your market. There is a strong correlation between the level of the faithful relationship existing between boss and team, with the market inputs that flow in. When faith among members in the group and with the boss is weak, then either due to lack of motivation the team members do not work with eyes and ears open, or they won't be confident to convey the market developments promptly with transparency to their superior. Knowing market happenings is one of the key elements in the four-pronged approach we saw earlier.

Faith coiled up in internal strengths

- Faith in yourself.
- Faith with your team.
- Faith in your product.
- Backing your team to fight with the sales-promotional tools at the command.

Faith in self and team

As a leader, you must have faith in your abilities and your team's capabilities to start with. A great saint of 20th century commonly referred to as Paramacharya from Tamil Nadu, India said:

Humans are one of the greatest creations of Almighty. That is why after demise, we pay homage to the body and respectfully pray for it to settle with Almighty.

The reference point here is humans are one of the greatest creations of the Lord. Thus, faith in oneself as a creation of Almighty becomes a must. For the same reason, seeing others as great creations of the Lord also becomes a must. This helps us move with love, care and consideration to others. Having faith in oneself thinking to oneself that he is a great creation of the Lord is the starting point. Many people may stop here. From here you need to expand appreciating your fellow humans too are the Lord's great creations. On the foundation of faith in oneself and his team members, a leader should move forward with the faith on many other things of relevance. If there is a sin I can think of avoiding at any cost, it is in not appreciating you as a great creation of Almighty. From this will emanate confidence, good behaviour and all the positives that have to come out of you. The moment you feel inferior or any negativity in you remind yourself that you are Lord's great creation. This imprint that one is a great creation of Almighty has to get into your mind, nerves and muscles.

A leader has to exhibit faith as his core trait in all the four pillars of support, namely KDA to guideline objectives; KDA to customer needs and market inputs; and KDA to internal strengths.

Faith in the product

First, sell the product to yourself and your team before trying it in the market. One should know one's product and its quality aspects and be convinced of it. A leader having this faith is crucial for mobilizing others to sell. For instance, if even by slip of the tongue you talk poorly about your product, it can become a virus affecting your team, by making them feel your product is not worth it, and thereby lose the gumption to push for its right price. It can be argued, for example, by a cement-industry professional that his product fares less in strength test in comparison with one or more of the competing products, and that it is difficult for him to repose faith in his product. In such cases, my view is: a product is positioned at a certain level it deserves based on the relative merits of the products available in the market. After this exercise, the faith required should follow for a leader and his team to fight it out in the market.

Use of sales-promotional tools on hand

As seen earlier, sales activities aim immediate results; marketing activities lay a platform for future results. All firms are not blessed with a separate marketing function in the building-material industry. In many firms, a sales function leader has to take care of sales and marketing needs. In such cases, the field-level people need to focus 90% of their work on immediate results and 10% of their time on work, which helps them in the future. A sales leader has to spend, say, 70% of his work on immediate result and 30% on helping the future performance. If a separate marketing function exists, then the entire sales team can devote over 90% of their time and energy on sales activities.

Since the entire team is involved in results, a sales leader is better off to involve the team and decide what sales promotion mix they can have for different markets within the budget, and then back the team to get full returns of the promotional activities. When deciding the "sales promotion mix", consideration is required for a balance between immediate results and future results. Too much focus on immediate results will cause shredding extra discounts which are not good for future brand value; too little focus on immediate needs and taking up large-scale marketing activities hoping for "future fortune" can be catastrophic. The schemes laid must be balanced having an eye on future improvement in brand equity. Marketing-service officials can take care of the commercial side of the marketing and sales-promotional activities so that the sales team can focus more on selling related activities. The sales promotion, and the strategic mix of it, must always start only after knowing the market dynamics and customer profiles.

Why need to have faith in sales promotions:

The sales promotions in building-material industry have two portions: one is the incentive portion given to the distribution/influence channel, and the other is the product promotion to a targeted audience who are already or possible future consumers.

In the FMCG industry when sales promotions are done, the focus is on attracting the individual end customer. Example: buy three, but pay for two, and the likes we come across daily. In the building-material industry, the focus is more on attracting the network, influencers and to use their ability for improving sales. This focus shows why distribution channels and influencers are the key links, for the industry, which explains the importance they command.

Philip Kotler, the marketing guru, reflected the growing importance that sales promotions command due to the growing need for immediate results. He observed in the late '70s in the United States, the advertisements vis-à-vis sales promotion expenditure ratio was 60:40 in the FMCG industry. Decades later, the ratio had changed to 35:65 in favour of sales promotion. When the number of products increases, alternatives is plenty in the market, there is a need to attract and influence immediate sales. In such contexts activities of sales promotions play an important role.

For the incentive part of sales promotions, the deciding factors can be as follows:

- 'Profitability' of the distribution channel.
- 'Togetherness' of the distribution channel with the company.

- Immediate or short-term (up to 1 year) plans with the network, to improve sales volumes.
- Moderate and adjust sales push, in line with the change in momentum in the market, which can be for many reasons such as seasonal weather changes, fall in demand, natural calamity such as rains, floods and political changes.
- Handle the price positioning envisaged in a particular market.
- To try and keep up the spirit of the distribution channel and influencers.

The following are some additional reasons why a firm needs sales promotions to extract sales volumes.

- When the market has more than two or three established brands with equally good brand recall, quality and features, then sales-promotional effectiveness acts as the decider for the increase in sales.
- With the proliferation in TV channels, the focus of channels has narrowed down to beam events, films and plays separately for different interest groups, regions, language, etc. With this development, the number of viewers of a channel has come down over the years. The number of programs that is of common interest to all has come down and hence advertising in those channels has become more expensive.
- There is an ever-growing culture to mute the TV when advertisements are beamed – I am one among them.
- On the other hand, sales promotions can be used flexibly to a precise set of customers.
- Sales promotions can be used imaginatively to set right any gap in relation or knowledge or communication that exists between the company and the consumers in a particular location.
- A sales-promotional program is two-way communication between the company and the audience. The feedback acquired

with interactive discussions can be used to rectify any shortcomings.

Sales promotion programs help in some specific situations such as the following:

- During product extensions to introduce, explain a new product features to the target audience.
- When a company adopts a new method of the sales process or had developed software or mobile applications etc. to communicate effectively in descriptive ways and to address doubts that may arise.

Advertisements coupled with sales promotions have a better impact than advertisements without sales promotion support. Let us see a possible situation to explain this.

Example: A company "ABC" was purchased by a market leader firm "DEF" which did not operate earlier in the territory operated by ABC. After acquisition, DEF decides to introduce its brand in the territory of ABC replacing that of ABC. DEF adopted the following approach in the market in this scenario:

- It advertised extensively on the TV, radio and print media covering that territory.
- Conducted event programs and also launched advertisements through distribution network.
- Announced a coupon scheme for end consumers; a lucky draw for 200 consumers per month, keeping an incentive range, and fixed a lucky draw date.
- The localized sales-promotional program and TV advertisements ran parallel during the period.
- Conducted periodic events in the territory to announce the lucky draw winners and published it in the print media the next day.

- Gave gifts to the distribution channel as a token of appreciation apart from the discounts announced.
- The results were very encouraging with a surge in sales.

This is a classic example when TV advertisements and sales promotion combined having a greater effect on getting improved results.

Faith in the sales promotion schemes and programs undertaken will become stronger if the performance of the activities is monitored.

For deciding the sales promotion mix for next term, a leader must have analysed the performance of the set of schemes of the existing term. Without having a measuring mechanism in place sales-promotion schemes will become like a freebee making the leader and his team members lose faith in it. The area in which the schemes are to be monitored should be based on the objectives for which they were conducted.

Some of the important factors to measure can be:

- Increase in sales volumes.
- Improvement in network numbers.
- Improvement in sales inquiries in the retail counter.
- Improvement in repeat purchase numbers.
- Increase in the number of influencers, for the brand.
- Improvement in the collection period.
- Reduction in demand for price cuts – in other words, improvement in product acceptability for its price.
- Improvement in the loyalty of the distribution network with the company.
- If the brand had to overcome any difficulty in product characteristics, to verify the improvement after addressing the issue.

If the answers are analysed, and based on the findings, if the schemes for next term are to be planned, then the leader and his team's confidence will be even better in the next term.

To summarize a leader must be an epitome of faith and confidence reflecting in all walks of his work.

FREEDOM

I shall bring here two areas of freedom – external and internal. External freedom is the freedom in the office atmosphere, whereas internal freedom is the mental freedom that helps you as a leader to attain great heights.

Freedom in environment

Freedom to perform, encouraging two-way communications, freedom to decide within one's limits, plan travel to accommodate results – all these convey a constructive atmosphere for bringing results. A tensed office impedes thinking creatively and sharing knowledge. It stunts development. People are of different kinds, some interact more and some given a chance are loners, but the spirit of freedom must exist within the team, for which the leader plays a key role by setting the tone himself.

Freedom of thought, speech and actions electrify the use of four pillars – a commitment to guideline objectives, serving customer needs, extracting market inputs, utilization of the team's internal strength – to its full potential.

Business strategists' burn midnight oil to figure out means and methods to figure out success formulae that competitors cannot copy. I feel the firm which has developed teams that can adhere to the four pillars based on faith and freedom as a culture will be hard to beat for any competitor. This I say because this is 360-degree coverage guided by faith and freedom which, if a competitor has to copy, he has to change the entire set up, which will take time.

Adhering and achieving guideline objectives need people to communicate freely of their feedback, to make requests for any adjustments for course corrections. If a customer issue crops up for service needs, freedom to express the requirement is a basic requirement. In the cement industry, when some good customers fail to give feedback about a recurring problem, and silently switch to a competitive brand, some main factors were found to be:

- If they communicate an issue to the company, the local field executive gets pulled up by seniors.
- Feedback more often created a tensed, tough climate to the local company official in his company and hence they avoid escalating the issue.

If you look at a micro-level the issue is one of lack of freedom for the official and (or) for the dealer network, directly or indirectly.

Negative activities, such as vindictiveness, informal groups based on race, religion, caste, language, and region; pulling people in public, do not help people exercise freedom of speech and actions.

A culture of freedom helps in employees appreciating, communicating, sharing and adjusting themselves with others to achieve guideline objectives. It helps both employees and distribution networks to communicate their ideas, issues, requirements; supplementary service needs, albeit freely, which can benefit the company and its bondage with the customers.

Freedom-oriented environment makes employees to be proactive in the market to dig out market inputs which form the core of many important decisions. It helps them to apply internal strengths such as product, sales promotions and services with a spirit and cooperativeness, which can improve productivity and improve brand image.

Internal Freedom: Mental freedom for a leader

What is freedom?

For an individual at its highest plateau of evolvement, mental freedom is a state when one is insulated from success getting into the head and failure resulting in depression. In other words, if we can work hard towards a goal and after achievement or failure, think "what next" and go about the next step or corrective action as the case may be, we are in the path of freedom. Instead, if we lose balance with success or failure, we need to regulate ourselves.

Our attachments to results help us act towards the results, but the very attachments bring misery too. Our attachments bring us joy and happiness, but along with it bring misery. But the challenge is we need to be happy and yet not carry this misery.

What is the solution then?

We need to act, to work with all our might, to persevere towards the goals, but we do not want misery. The world will be a lot better if only we know to avoid misery, yet able to act well. The self-drive, striving for results, passion for the job and such attachments which help us work more are temperamental assets, dam good to have, provided we know how to add a rider to them. The truth is, selfish people will remain unhappy; even if they manage to get physical assets, glorified designations and comforts. Unselfish ones have their gates open for happiness.

How to unravel this paradox?

To me, the best solution lies in taking a strong conviction that we shall plan for results based on the **common good**. Then for the common good let us go after the result. Whatever personal benefit and riches that accrues because of the achievements let it be a by-product. Never take credit for the fruits of your actions to your mind, because in all actions others would have played a part, directly or indirectly. This is a huge challenge. For example, we often witness situations when people after a laudable performance expect appreciations to pour on them. Our mind is trained from childhood to think this way and hence with practice alone, it can be overcome and not overnight.

We need to make a deep dive into our origin – How we came into the world? Who we are in reality? By doing this we can get one thing clear; we did not get this body ourselves. Theists can consider their body and life as the Almighty's work. The atheists may consider it as a work of nature but cannot deny that they did not create their body and infused life in it. For theists, to acquire humility in not taking credit to their actions is relatively easy as they can credit it to the Lord – since they accept their body and life is a gift from the Almighty. Theists can well appreciate that they indeed do not have the rights to take credit for the fruits of their actions. For atheists, it takes mental maturity to give the credit to nature after accepting their birth is an act of nature.

Either way, if we can give up the thought of taking credit for the fruits of our actions we avoid misery. Mental misery comes when you expect personal returns. Our business is to act, act with spirit and soul, and only that much and no further of crediting ourselves. On the other hand, this habit brings in such a balance of mind unaffected by success and failure, which we call mental freedom. In that state, we can think better for the right solutions, talk with humility and take actions that will benefit all. Instead, if one works hard to achieve success, only to credit oneself for achievement, then his character takes a descending path and stands to lose his achievements in the long run. Moreover, such people will get extremely distressed during a period of failures.

Such people will swing between good mood and unhappiness because they have become slaves of their successes and failures as they take credit for their actions and results. This is what Swami

Vivekananda refers to when he asks us to live as masters and not as slaves.

Real happiness is a state when we are insulated from being affected by pleasure and pain. Pleasure and pain will have a physical effect on us, as they arise from the senses. But our mood depends on what thoughts we pass on to the mind and not on what happens around us.

When a leader acts with freedom, he can be infectious on his fellow teammates. He will be a person to look up to in crunch situations, and they will be confident too to be transparent, as they expect the leader to be unselfish as he had planned the results for the common good.

HARD WORK

Countless occasions in our life we have heard of the importance of hard work. Like preaching on the need of god worship and ways of worship, the repeated encouragement to work hard from all corners suggests, most people are not consistent in doing it. Similar to God's worship, hard work also can be explained and detailed in a countless number of ways with the hope that in one way or another at some point of time in life the truth behind the need to work hard will catch up with people. A leader has to be a benchmark of hard work to his direct reports, as then only he has the best chance of influencing his team to put their shoulders to the wheel and work with purpose tirelessly.

Sales professionals tend to correlate hard work with only fieldwork and stop there. I dare say, hard work means using both body and mind. A sales professional who works tirelessly in the field, but without improving his knowledge base at the required pace will stagnate after some time. For those who want to correlate hard work and career growth and verify its value, I have some views to share.

1. Some people work hard and grow high on the ladder in professional life.
2. Some work hard, but grow only to reasonable levels.
3. Some don't work hard but get into good positions.
4. Some due to lack of hard work decline and fall out.

Of the above four possibilities, I give the highest probability of occurrence to first and fourth in the above list. To me, almost all who got to the top and remained there had the signature of hard work in their lives. Those who by fortune or influence get into good positions without the drive to work hard fall out in due course. Due to misfortune or other life balancing considerations, some people who work hard may end up at the median level in positions. For these people in my view at least hard work will ensure two things – they will not be failures in career; they will be mentally happy with themselves, if they realise the cause.

What is hard work will vary as per the roles that are undertaken. For a sales leader, it is manifold – physical, mental and psychological. For a labourer, hard work has a lot to do with physical labour. For a professor, it has to do with increasing his subject knowledge and making students well versed with it and so on. According to the responsibility, one is endowed with, in a job the meaning of the term hard work will differ.

Index to self-introspection: When work comes forth, if the first reaction of mind thinks of the pain of work then it is time to introspect oneself. For instance, a hard-working architect should not think twice for thinking creatively; an analyst should not consider it a pain to rock forward and backward with numbers and facts; a politician should not consider understanding people issues as pain. If this happens one has to encourage and correct oneself. Many times we miss listening to our behaviour and our reactions – physical and mental, to various events that unfold to us.

A sales leader should be ready for physical work which includes visiting the markets; mental efforts to unearth knowledge, analyse, understand and reflect wisdom. The psychological part of his hard work is to put to control his mind and not be reactive. For many, the psychological aspect may be the hardest to do, and hence, they need to earnestly explore into themselves. I get reminded of Swami Vivekananda's description of Lord's incarnations, born at various stages of history across the world to help humanity. He said such incarnations to him appeared to be great personalities who brought in a wonderful combination of "mind, heart and hand" in all their actions. Greatness in mind and heart involves hard work with the mind and application of values; greatness in hand involves iterative practice bringing skill and finesse in physical activities. *In short, it is all hard work*. Except for our birth and love of parents, nothing can be acquired free and easy in life – this is the hard fact of life.

If a sales leader has to excel in the four pillars of performance detailed earlier, he should embrace hard work. Slippage can happen here and there. Sheer exhaustion, occasional outbursts, and mistiming can happen – for all are humans, and bound to slip. But a leader who strives consciously to practice the four founding principles described here will know he is getting off track and this will help him recoup himself back on right track. A sales leader who puts his heart and soul for becoming an expert in his domain will be a welcome personality in the market, friends, colleagues, direct reports and seniors. Putting heart and soul for expertise is hard work.

Harsha Bhogle, the popular cricket commentator, in his book "The Winning Way" gives a reference of a cricket captain's address to his team, which can give us an important insight. The captain is reported to have told his team that winning and losing are part of the game and that the captain understands that no team can win all of its matches. But what the captain did not want was a loss caused due to a lack of effort by the team.

EMBRACING PEOPLE

When "by the people" is the truth; "for the people" must be the foundation. Business entities are run by the people. Hence, undertaking activities, keeping people in mind become a concrete foundation.

Embracing people for guideline factors

The sales head needs to get his needs to be approved at the CEO level in the course of achieving guideline objectives. For sales promotions, marketing budgets, manpower requirements, training requirements and getting major approvals sanctioned, things have to move through senior people from other departments. Having good relations and knowing how to go about the various tasks through them, both are important. It can be argued that a CEO needs to give approvals in the company's interests and what could be the special need for a sales head in getting approvals. The key is to enable C suite brass to appreciate the needs of the sales department. For this, the head of sales has to put things across in right perspective after knowing what the CEO's focus areas are.

In a particular year, the focus may be on increasing the brand equity, while in another phase the focus might be to quicken cash inflows. A CEO may be number savvy and people development-oriented. These requirements can be known only with close interactions and maintaining close links with the top brass. This implies getting into the good books of right men at the top is important for chief of sales.

A middle-level sales leader has to interact with peers in other departments such as finance, logistics and human resource. Since customer needs have to be satisfied taking services from other departments, and since it is the sales team which is going to face the customer, it is prudent to keep close and mutually respectful relationships with people from other departments.

Relationship with finance heads

When it comes to money the factors which command the greatest respect are its increased returns and reduced risks. When a leader has done the homework on why and how he has planned sales-promotional incentives, expenditures, etc. having an evaluation of past returns and future expected returns will help to get clearances.

As sales professionals, you might know even by gut feel what can be the impact of a sales promotion scheme on sales volumes, but you cannot expect a finance person to appreciate the importance of the sales promotion scheme in the same way. Finance people go by numbers and as much as possible as a sales leader, you should quantify soft factors to make your claims appeal to finance heads. You both may have the same objectives for the company, but exposure, approaches and evaluating methods differ. For other aspects of the requirements of your department, go as much as possible with numbers.

Credibility must be given importance as finance heads give high priority for numbers. If two sales schemes have an outgo of $50,000, if the corresponding revenue had increased by $1m, with a 10% margin, you need to bring this to the light of the finance department. Such culture can help in future approvals, as it will be known that you plan with clarity on returns and have a method of measuring the returns.

Interactions with HR

For HR the factors, such as the happiness of people, reduced labour turnover, the utility of training undertaken, reduced absenteeism, improved productivity per person, are the key focus areas.

If you have a tracking mechanism of your team's meticulous fieldwork with tour plans followed, daily feedbacks submitted then it is good to apprise HR of these as it will help during annual appraisals.

One of the best ways of earning your subordinates confidence in you as a leader is to tell HR of the employees' positives in the employee's presence when opportunities arise.

During the annual appraisals to follow the timelines, details and coverage are important, as the HR personnel will be racing against timelines for consolidation and interpretation of the appraisal forms.

Interactions with the CEO

With CEOs the commodity they are always short of is time. In case of one-to-one interactions with CEOs, you need to be as precise, clear and crisp as possible. If you know the interaction in advance do some homework on possible areas of discussions and in those areas be ready with figures, facts and explanations.

When it comes to presentations, the same principles of clarity in figures, reliability of data and facts apply. Explanations supporting presentations need to be crisp, precise with proper diplomatic language. Positivity by way of constructive thoughts and a summary of the objectives of the presentation will give the edge. Make a mock trial of the presentation a few times well before, for spontaneity and flow in communications. At any point in time, it should reflect that you know what is happening under you.

Embracing people upstream

As a sales leader, you should not have any inhibitions in the dealings with customers. A leader cannot know all customers' profiles in detail, but you need to be familiar with at least the top 20% who account for 80% revenue or volumes. In case of any bottlenecks or issues as a leader, you must be in a position to talk, mediate and resolve. For this, you must be a person who cares, loves, easily approachable and takes a fair stand.

During any sales-promotional presentations, promotional programs with the customer base, you must allocate as much time for interactive sessions. After any feedback, to follow it up and make the customer know about it and changes effected will lift you and company's image. It will set the tone and culture for team members to lift themselves if required. If you have details of the performance of the network and their capabilities use it in conversations for strengthening your relationship.

One area where leaders get into a trap with customers, which is their own making, is on the emotional aspect or ego which leads to giving false promises. It will be tempting to develop a conversation with promises, but if you cannot keep your promise, then it will affect your credibility and image in the long run. It can also end up influencing your direct reports to commit the same error in the future. In your heart, you have to take up a resolve to take care of customers. That is the key. In communications and interactions without falling trap to emotions try best to be empathetic and give diplomatic commitments, coupled with thoroughness in actions and keep them appraised. This will do wonders in the long run than being full of promises in interactions and then not living up to it.

Embracing people to use internal strengths and manage markets

Well known but less realized and applied by the mind is the truth that sales force ultimately works alone in the field to get cash flow for the company. One may have the best of products, support, promotions, but to convert these assets into cash every member of the field team is a transacting force. Banks lend money, which has to be returned with interest. Customers bring in money which has profit stored inside. The field force is the one lever that brings this cash. To keep them in the right frame of mind is very crucial to make them be proactive in their work and improve cash flows. A sales leader takes the lead in this initiative.

Unlike what you may have with the staff from other departments as a sales spearhead you have many things in common with the team under you and try to fully appreciate that. Both you and the team want sales growth. All decisions for your interactions with the sales team should have this thumb rule. Here the word "interactions" is the key. Interactions include all your communications – oral and written, with people under you.

Caution needs to be applied while communicating; no lethargy of mind needs to be allowed during communications. Lethargy of mind is a villain. It sows the seed to speak with loose words without application of the principles you believe in, which will end up communicating what you don't intend to. Later to correct the situation, after spilling wrong words, you may have to take a lot of effort which can be avoided, if only you remain alert when you communicate with your team.

If an action is going to bring down business, avoid doing it. If it helps business growth, act upon it. At the end of the month, sales staff gets maximum satisfaction in achieving the targets. If you as a leader helped them to achieve it, you have done it right yet again. Ask yourself three questions when you handle sales staff down the line – "Have I helped them to use their time efficiently?", "Have I energized them?" and "Have I helped them towards targets?"

When dealing with people down the line, focus need be on things common between you. Please avoid raking up issues which are not common, for example, your issue with an operations department, etc. Personal interactions, which are mutually helpful; sales, volumes, relationships, collections, effective sales promotions, service improvements, solving any pending issues etc., are the areas to focus.

Apply a business model for targets and territories: When you fix targets and territories to people fairness and reality are required. If targets have unfairness built-in, then whatever motivation you try to build with the team member will be looked with a sceptical mind. Many times top management gives targets, which gets divided based on convenience or historical data.

Targets can be a combination of volumes, collection, increase in customer base, call numbers, sales promotion events, service improvements, solving pending issues, etc. Apply factors such as competition level, profitability, network strength, age of your brand, acceptability level in the market, sales promotion support, demand dynamics of the market, the time required for increasing customer base and travel time required between calls.

Motivation of team: Two factors which will pay dividends in motivation are:

- Understand what motivates a person: From your experience, interactions, inferences try your best to know what motivates the individual. If you can help him in his mission consistently, it acts as a boost to motivate and builds confidence in you. Helping someone in his life goals is care that flows from the heart. When the goal of the team member is within the frame of work and legitimate – which passes the test of ethics – lend a helping hand.

- Encourage the individual: You cannot encourage a person genuinely unless you have applied your mind to know a person. From the interactions with a person try to assimilate his genuine strengths. Then explain to him, the value of his strengths and encourage. Understanding what motivates a person and encouraging his strength will be useful for your employees in the way they handle customers, as they can apply this habit with customers which can improve their productivity.

Encouraging and motivating others have a clear possibility of you sharpening your positive mentality. This I say because unless you see the positives in a person you cannot tell him what factors are good with him. By developing the habit of seeing the positives in others you are developing yourself as a positive-minded motivator. In due course of time, you will be a leader approached by others for their self-development.

Ultimately, it can have a cyclic effect. A well-motivated and supported staff can be expected to be more productive, applying the four pronged approach, and sustain their position as performers.

CONCLUSION

With non-negotiable qualities that act as an underlying force, you bring out excellence with the four-pronged approach from yourself and the team. This marks the making of a leader who sets an example, as a benchmark of sorts for others. As a result, you as a leader by way of moulding your mind, personality and functions attain greatness in job functions and as an excellent human being, for life.

Dr E Ravishankar would be happy to be reached at:
eravishankar.at@gmail.com**; Mobile: +91 7871267799**